Public Health Leadership

Designed for professionals and aspiring professionals in public policy, public health, and related programs, *Public Health Leadership* illustrates the complexity of contemporary issues at the intersection of public health and healthcare and the compelling need to engage numerous public and private stakeholders to effectively advance population health. Offering real-world case studies and cutting-edge topics in public health and healthcare, this book will complement existing primers and introductory books in public health to help students and practitioners bridge concepts and practice.

The work is divided into three parts that focus on the new role of public health departments, emerging challenges and opportunities following the enactment of the Patient Protection and Affordable Care Act (ACA), and recent trends in innovation and investment. Each chapter is practice-oriented to provide insight into the changing landscape of public health while offering practical tips based on the experiences and expertise of leading practitioners. Topics include cross-sector partnership-building, innovations in investment strategies, public health operations, performance management, advances in big data tracking, and more that address the social determinants of health and improve population health. Cases draw on a wide range of perspectives and regions, encouraging the reader, whether a professional or student, to apply the lessons learned to one's local context.

Richard F. Callahan is Professor and former Chair of the Department of Public and Nonprofit Administration at the University of San Francisco, USA.

Dru Bhattacharya is Director of the Master of Public Health Program and Chair of the Department of Population Health Sciences in the School of Nursing and Health Professions at the University of San Francisco, USA.

Public Health Leadership

Strategies for Innovation in
Population Health and
Social Determinants

Edited by Richard F. Callahan
and Dru Bhattacharya

NEW YORK AND LONDON

First published 2017
by Routledge
605 Third Avenue, New York, NY 10017

and by Routledge
4 Park Square, Milton Park, Abingdon, Oxon OX14 4RN

First issued in paperback 2022

Routledge is an imprint of the Taylor & Francis Group, an informa business

© 2017 Taylor & Francis

Publisher's Note
The publisher has gone to great lengths to ensure the quality of this reprint but points out that some imperfections in the original copies may be apparent.

Library of Congress Cataloging in Publication Data
Names: Callahan, Richard F., 1959- editor. | Bhattacharya, Dru, editor.
Title: Public health leadership : strategies for innovation in population health and social determinants / edited by Richard F. Callahan and Dru Bhattacharya.
Description: New York : Routledge, 2016. | Includes bibliographical references and index.
Identifiers: LCCN 2016029946| ISBN 9781498760768 (hardback : alk. paper) | ISBN 9781315405827 (ebook)
Subjects: | MESH: Public Health Administration--methods | Leadership | Organizational Case Studies | Health Status Disparities | United States
Classification: LCC RA425 | NLM WA 540 AA1 | DDC 362.1--dc23
LC record available at https://lccn.loc.gov/2016029946

ISBN 13: 978-1-03-247698-8 (pbk)
ISBN 13: 978-1-4987-6076-8 (hbk)
ISBN 13: 978-1-315-40582-7 (ebk)

DOI: 10.4324/9781498760768

Typeset in Sabon
by Saxon Graphics Ltd, Derby

Contents

Acknowledgments

Rich Callahan would like to thank each of the authors for their contributions to this book, for their discussions with me, for their presentations in leadership programs, and for their long-standing commitments to improving the lives of others. In particular: Dr. Kenneth Kizer, Jon Freedman, Chet Hewitt, Dr. Robert Ross, Dr. Anthony Iton, and Lavonna Blair Lewis – and special thanks to my co-editor, Dru. I am also indebted to the late Grantland Johnson for his discussions with me, as well as his lifetime of work addressing the social determinants of health before the term came into common use. I want to thank Fr. James Hanvey, S.J. for the opportunity to work on this book and spend a term at Campion Hall, Oxford University, and Troy Ellerman for his helpful proofreading and editing, as well as my supportive colleagues at the University of San Francisco, including President Steve Privett and President Paul Fitzgerald, along with Deans Mike Duffy, Mike Webber, and Liz Davis, and Judy Karshmer, as well as Tony Ribera and Catherine Horiuchi. And my thanks to my wife, Denise, and my sons, Daniel and David.

Dru Bhattacharya would like to extend his gratitude to each author for the depth of inquiry and deliberation on so many pressing issues, and particularly Rich for his guidance, leadership, and wisdom. I would like to also thank Dr. Ajay K. Singh, Senior Associate Dean for Global and Continuing Education at Harvard Medical School, for his mentorship during my studies in clinical epidemiology at Harvard and the heightened training in team-based learning, which enabled me to appreciate the balance of planning and implementation. I want to thank Kathryn Hall-Trujillo, former public health administrator for the state of California, founder of the Birthing Project USA, and CNN Hero-of-the-Year recipient, whose wisdom, guidance, and support has been indispensable in shaping my creativity in our ongoing collaborative efforts. And heartfelt thanks to my parents, Dr. Pranab and Indira Bhattacharya; my wife, Christina, for her unwavering support; and our children, Stephanie, Domenico, Serafina, and Cecilia.

About the Editors

Richard F. Callahan, Professor, University of San Francisco.

Dr. Callahan's research, teaching, and practice focus on leadership behaviors and strategies that are effective in complex, demanding, and dynamic environments in the public and nonprofit sectors. At the University of San Francisco Callahan is a Professor, having chaired the Department of Public and Nonprofit Administration. He served three years as the Faculty representative to the USF Board of Trustees, and was Director for the *Change the World From Here* lecture series at USF.

Starting in 2000, Callahan has been Co-Director of the Sierra Health Foundation Leadership program, currently with Dr. Kenneth W. Kizer. Over the past twenty-five years he has worked with the executive team of the Los Angeles County Department of Public Health, as well as elected and appointed officials in state and local government across a range of departments. His recent service includes acting as Executive Producer of the documentary *Solving the Inequality*. He has received a Fulbright Specialist Program grant for lectures and curriculum design in Istanbul, Turkey. He has designed and delivered leadership and training programs internationally, nationally, state-wide, and regionally, as well as being co-designer of the University of Southern California's Executive Master of Leadership degree.

Callahan co-authored a national award-winning article, receiving the Brownlow Award for Best Article from *Public Administration Review*. He has been published in journals including *Public Administration Review*, *Public Management Review*, *Public Manager*, *American Review of Public Administration*, *Government Finance Officers Review*, *The National Civic Review*, and *Journal of Jesuit Business Education*. As a teacher in graduate programs, he was awarded Teacher of the Year 2013 in the USF School of Management, and the University of Southern California School of Policy Graduate Programs Academic Community Teacher of the Year in 2010 and 2007. He received his BA from Georgetown University and a Master's degree and Doctorate from the University of Southern California.

Dru Bhattacharya is Director, Master of the Public Health Program and Chair of the Department of Population Health Sciences in the School of Nursing and Health Professions, University of San Francisco.

"Professor Dru", as his students refer to him, is an interdisciplinary public health researcher and practitioner. He was the first (and only) J.D. selected to participate in and successfully complete the post-doctoral Global Clinical Scholars Research Training Program through Harvard University Medical School, with advanced training in clinical epidemiology. He received his advanced training in law from Georgetown University Law Center (LL.M., with distinction), and his Master of Public Health in health policy and finance from Johns Hopkins Bloomberg School of Public Health, where he also obtained a Certificate in Maternal and Child Health.

Professor Dru is also the author of two books on domestic and global policy, and has been consulted to inform the creation of doctoral programs in public health policy and advocacy based on his expertise. His textbook, *Public Health Policy: Issues, Theories, and Advocacy*, has also been adopted by institutions with core classes in public health policy, and is notable for distinguishing the fields, and its purpose, from healthcare policy generally, promoting his unique "PEEEL" framework, drawing from the disciplines of politics, epidemiology, ethics, economics, and law to advance public health policy analysis and decision-making.

Professor Dru has delivered over eighty-three invited presentations across the nation and at international conferences. Prior to joining USF he was a founding Director of the public health policy program at Loyola University Chicago, a Fellow at the Centers for the Law and the Public's Health at Johns Hopkins Bloomberg School of Public Health, and a Congressional staffer serving under former Chairman Henry Waxman of the Committee on Oversight and Government Reform in the U.S. Congress House of Representatives while assisting counsel investigate a global health project gone awry. He has collaborated with local, state, and national partners in conducting multi-state legal assessments of health-related laws, drafting model health legislation, and conducting health policy analyses of existing or proposed interventions to improve healthcare delivery and promote population health.

He is currently collaborating with partners in health departments and private practitioners to explore the role of medical-legal partnerships as a locus of research and intervention to alleviate health disparities among vulnerable populations. He has held over nine editorial positions, was a former Board Member of the Public Health Lawyers Association, and currently serves on the MLP Advisory Committee for the Illinois Supreme Court Access to Justice Commission, conducting research to advance the mission of the Commission to promote the role of the MLPs across Illinois to reduce health disparities. His education includes a Certificate in Clinical Epidemiology from Harvard University Medical School, LLM from Georgetown University Law Center; MPH from Johns Hopkins University, and a BA in Biology from the University of Chicago.

About the Contributors

Jay Bhatt, D.O., MPH, MPA, FRCP, is the Chief Medical Officer of the American Hospital Association, and President and CEO of the Health Research & Educational Trust (HRET), overseeing the American Hospital Association's clinical leadership and health activities. Dr. Bhatt leads the AHA's quality activities in HRET, and the Institute for Diversity in Health Management and Association for Health Improvement, and also directs physician engagement activities and provide leadership on policy issues. Prior to joining the AHA, he served as the Chief Health Officer of the Illinois Hospital Association where he lead activities of the Institute for Innovations Care and Quality to reduce readmissions and patient harms, which resulted in the prevention of 15,887 instances of patient harm for cost savings of $161 million, and significant reduction in falls, blood clots, early elective deliveries. He also developed physician engagement and alignment strategies that included the Medical Executive Forum, Health Care System Physician Forum, and Physician Leadership Academy, which represents 15,000 physicians and 1000 engaged through learning and action networks. He also served as member of the Executive Leadership Team of the Association helping manage budget of $50 million and 150 employees. Dr. Bhatt is also a Clinical Fellow in Medicine with Harvard Medical School.

Jonathan Freedman is Managing Principal of Health Management Associates, a leading independent national research and consulting firm. He was previously Chief Strategy Officer, L.A. Care Health Plan, the largest publicly operated health plan in the nation. Prior to joining L.A. Care Health Plan, Mr. Freedman held a variety of management and leadership roles for more than twenty-five years with the County of Los Angeles, most recently as Chief Deputy Director of the Los Angeles County Department of Public Health (DPH). Other roles included managing Los Angeles County's state and federal legislative programs, directing the Medicaid Demonstration Project for Los Angeles County, and serving as an Assistant Deputy for health, welfare and environmental issues to Supervisor Ed Edelman, a former member of the Los Angeles County Board of Supervisors.

Mr. Freedman has extensive experience in public health, safety net health care, and public policy. He has led many high-profile initiatives, including the public health response to the 1994 Northridge earthquake, Los Angeles County's Master Tobacco Settlement negotiation, solutions to funding crises in the Los Angeles County safety net, and the 2010 H1N1 influenza response.

Mr. Freedman has received outstanding leadership awards from California State Association of Counties and Los Angeles County. His work has been published in *Health Affairs*, and he is a contributor to *Public Health Practice: What Works* published by Oxford University Press. Mr. Freedman holds a Bachelor's degree in Political Science and a Master's degree in Public Health from UCLA.

Chet P. Hewitt is the President and CEO of Sierra Health Foundation and its independent operating unit, the Center for Health Program Management, which he founded in 2012. Since beginning his tenure at the foundation in 2007, Chet has focused foundation investments in four areas: health disparities, social determinants of health, health care access, and the well-being of vulnerable youth populations. Known for his collaborative leadership style, innovative approach to program design and management, and willingness to take thoughtful risk, Chet has increased the foundation's influence, reach and impact.

Prior to joining the foundation, Chet served for five years as the Director of Alameda County's Social Services Agency where he achieved national recognition for transforming its failing child welfare system into a national model and using technology to improve the management and accessibility of human service programs. Previously he served as Associate Director for the Rockefeller Foundation in New York, where he oversaw its national employment and community building initiatives, and Program Director for the Center on Juvenile and Criminal Justice in San Francisco where he founded its highly regarded Detention Diversion Advocacy Program. Chet has received several awards for his work, including the Robert T. Matsui Community Service Award, the Grantland Johnson Intergovernmental Cooperation Award, the Annie E. Casey Foundation Child and Family Leaders Fellowship, and the Black Administrators in Child Welfare's Child Welfare Administrator of the Year.

Chet is a frequent lecturer on philanthropy and public sector leadership, and has advised jurisdictions around the country on issues related to the transformation of public systems. Most recently he helped found and currently serves as a co-chair of the California Executives' Alliance, a consortium of twenty-two foundations focused on improving the life chances of boys and young men of color in

California, and launched the San Joaquin Valley Fund to spur health and well-being investment in one of California's most underfunded regions. Chet serves on several boards, including the Roberts Enterprise Development Fund, the Public Policy Institute of California, Valley Vision, and Sacramento Steps Forward. Born and raised in New York City, Chet credits life experience as the primary source of his commitment to serve those less fortunate than himself. He is driven by his desire to ensure that his two young sons, and all children, have every opportunity to grow up healthy, safe, and prepared for their roles as vital members of their communities.

Dr. Anthony Iton believes that reinvigorating democracy in California's underserved communities is the first step in improving residents' health. As Senior Vice President of the *Building Healthy Communities* program, Iton is leading an effort to empower residents in fourteen cities with the worst health outcomes across California to fight for changes in their communities that will help them lead healthier lives. When residents are engaged in holding elected officials accountable for fair educational opportunities, good jobs and more green space, Dr. Iton believes that good health can thrive. This place-based approach is founded on the idea that residents can't be asked to eat healthier food, exercise more, regularly visit the doctor, or get a better job if those opportunities aren't available in the communities where they live. The BHC model attacks the root causes of health inequities by convening and supporting community partners on the ground. By building resiliency and advocacy among residents, his work has made significant and sustainable advances in public health for thousands of Californians.

Prior to his appointment at the Endowment, Iton served as the director and County Health Officer for the Alameda County Public Health Department. Under his leadership, Alameda County launched an innovative plan to improve the health and lifespan of low-income communities by focusing on the poverty, racism, and discrimination that prevented residents from getting good housing, better jobs, and quality healthcare and educational opportunities. By inserting a public health perspective into conversations about community and economic development, he led the department's efforts to improve community engagement and galvanize equity-driven policy solutions aimed at improving residents' health.

Iton's dedication to improving the quality of people's lives was founded during his contrasted experiences growing up in Montreal, Canada and attending medical school in East Baltimore, Maryland. The health inequities that he witnessed in Baltimore were almost unimaginable in Montreal, inspiring Iton to pursue a career at the intersection of public health and social justice.

Published in numerous public health and medical publications, Iton is a regular public health lecturer and keynote speaker at conferences across the nation. He earned his B.S. in Neurophysiology, with honors, from McGill University in Montreal, Quebec, his J.D. at the University of California, Berkeley's Boalt Hall School of Law, and his medical degree from Johns Hopkins University School of Medicine.

The Honorable Kenneth W. Kizer, MD, MPH is a Distinguished Professor and Director of the Institute for Population Health Improvement at the University of California Davis. He is an internationally respected healthcare leader who has the very rare distinction of having been elected to the National Academy of Medicine and to the National Academy of Public Administration.

Dr. Kizer is a highly seasoned physician executive whose diverse professional experience includes senior positions in the public and private sectors, academia, and philanthropy. Among his previous positions are: founding CEO and President of the National Quality Forum, a Washington DC-based quality improvement and consensus standards-setting body that has been called the nation's premier health care quality improvement organization; Chairman, CEO and President of Medsphere Systems Corporation, a leading commercial provider of open source health information technology; Under Secretary for Health, U.S. Department of Veterans Affairs and chief executive officer of the nation's largest healthcare system, in which capacity he engineered the internationally acclaimed transformation of the Veterans Healthcare System in the late 1990s; Director of California Department of Health Services; and Director of California Emergency Medical Services Authority, where he was the architect of the state's EMS and trauma care systems in the early 1980s. During his record tenure as California's top health official he oversaw the state's response to the HIV/AIDS epidemic, pioneered Medicaid managed care, engineered California's famed Tobacco Control Program and the '5-a-Day' for Better Nutrition Program, restructured many of the state's public health programs, launched initiatives to improve the quality of nursing homes, and oversaw a dramatically enlarged toxic substances control program and the genesis of the California Environmental Protection Agency.

He has served on the U.S. Preventive Services Task Force and as Chairman of the California Wellness Foundation, the nation's largest philanthropic organization devoted exclusively to health promotion and disease prevention, as well as on the governing boards of a number of managed care and health IT companies, foundations, professional associations, and non-profit organizations. He has been an advisor to numerous foreign countries on health matters.

Dr. Kizer is an honors graduate of Stanford University and UCLA, the recipient of two honorary doctorates, and a fellow or distinguished fellow of eleven professional societies. He is board-certified in six medical specialties and/or subspecialties, and has authored over four hundred original articles, book chapters, and other reports. He is a Fellow National of the international Explorer's Club, a founding member and architect of the international Wilderness Medical Society, a former Navy diving medical officer, and a recognized expert on aquatic sports and wilderness medicine.

His accomplishments have been recognized with dozens of awards, and he has been selected as one of the '100 Most Powerful People in Healthcare' by *Modern Healthcare* magazine on several occasions. His work has been featured in *Time*, *Business Week*, *Fortune*, the *Wall Street Journal*, *New York Times*, and numerous other magazines, newspapers, and national television shows.

Lavonna Blair Lewis, PhD, MPH is a Teaching Professor of Public Policy, the Diversity Liaison at the USC Sol Price School of Public Policy, and the Director of the USC Diversity in Healthcare Leadership Initiative. Dr. Lewis joined the USC faculty in 1996 from Rice University where she received her PhD in Political Science. Dr. Lewis' areas of research and professional interests consistently focus on cultural competency and health disparities, targeting both the health status and healthcare needs of underrepresented groups. As such, she feels she has a two-fold mission in life—to make the invisible visible (if people are blind or unaware of problems for a particular group or in a particular community, you have to find ways to get these problems onto their radar) and to make people uncomfortable (she believes that if people are always comfortable, they aren't being challenged or they have quit learning and growing).

She is currently involved in multiple projects that address racial and ethnic health disparities in cardiovascular disease (CVD), diabetes, and infant mortality. Her work has appeared in the *American Journal of Public Health*, *Family and Community Health*, the *Journal of General Internal Medicine*, and other health management and policy journals. All of the work to date has employed a community-based participatory research framework that partners with the relevant stakeholder groups in developing the research questions.

Robert K. Ross, M.D. is President and Chief Executive Officer of the California Endowment, a private, statewide health foundation established in 1996 to address the health needs of Californians. Prior to his appointment in July 2000, Dr. Ross served as director of the Health and Human Services Agency for the County of San Diego from 1993 to 2000.

Dr. Ross has an extensive background in health philanthropy, as a public health administrator, and as a clinician. His service includes: Commissioner of the Philadelphia Department of Public Health; medical director for the LINK School-Based Clinic Program, Camden, New Jersey; instructor of clinical medicine, Children's Hospital of Philadelphia; and faculty member at San Diego State University's School of Public Health.

Dr. Ross has been actively involved in community and professional activities at both the local and national level. He is a member of the President's Advisory Commission on Educational Excellence for African Americans, Co-Chair of the Diversity in Philanthropy Coalition, and has served as a member of the California Health Benefit Exchange Board, the Rockefeller Philanthropy Advisors Board, the National Vaccine Advisory Committee, and on the boards of Grantmakers in Health, the National Marrow Donor Program, San Diego United Way, and Jackie Robinson YMCA. He is a Diplomate of the American Academy of Pediatrics, served on the President's Summit for America's Future and as chairman of the national Boost for Kids Initiative, and was honored by the Council on Foundations as the Distinguished Grantmaker of the Year for 2008. Dr. Ross received his undergraduate and Master's degrees in Public Administration and medical degrees from the University of Pennsylvania in Philadelphia.

The California Endowment makes grants to organizations and institutions that directly benefit the health and well-being of the people of California. For more information, visit our website at www.calendow.org.

Part I

Public Health Departments

Scope, Systems, and Standards

1 Introduction

Leadership Journeys to the Social Determinants of Health

Richard F. Callahan, DPA

I. Introduction

The road to addressing the social determinants of health can be a personal journey, leading to a professional impact. In the start of his most recent book, Michael Marmot (2015) recalls his experience as a young physician seeing patients and how he began questioning healthcare to better help individuals. My formal introduction to the social determinants of health began with conversations with Grantland Johnson, California's Health and Social Service Agency Secretary, in between talking about great baseball players. The discussion continued in depth when I was directing the Sierra Health Foundation Leadership and meeting with the newly appointed President and Chief Executive Officer, Chet Hewitt. In that initial conversation Chet suggested inviting Dr. Anthony Iton, the Public Health Officer of Alameda County and his former colleague in this urban county in the San Francisco Bay area, as a speaker to the leadership program.

In presenting to a leadership program of twenty-five nonprofit health executives, Dr. Iton captivated a group of experienced and emerging leaders with his extensive data analysis showing graphically that your zip code matters for more than your postal delivery. The social and economic factors affecting the neighborhood you live in profoundly affect your life-long health outcomes. I knew that place—neighborhoods, communities, specific locations—mattered on many levels, from my professional experience working on homelessness, children's protective services, and gang violence in Los Angeles County government (http://video.pbssocal.org/program/passion-and-politics-ed-edelman/), as well as academically in that governments create place value through institutions and organizations (Kirlin 1996) and in recent work on the impact of Hurricane Katrina (Gladwell 2015).

Dr. Iton's presentation extensively cited census tract level data, but never lost focus on the impact on individuals, families, and neighborhoods. Over the past five years Dr. Iton's discussion has evolved to begin with the fundamental questions of the social determinants of health: why do we tolerate the conditions in America where people live in the inner city? What are the socially created differences that impact the health outcomes for individuals in a census tract or zip code? These questions extend beyond traditional public health to look at income, education, housing, land use planning, politics, and other factors.

II. Social Determinants of Health and Population Health

Dr. Iton is not alone in asking these questions. Internationally, Marmot writes: "There has been considerable progress in the recognition and adoption of the social determinants of health approach to health equity" (Marmot and Allen 2014, S518). On the East Coast of the United States the Harlem Children's Zone represents a significant and long-standing investment recognizing and addressing the impact of the social determinants of health. On the West Coast, in California, a state generating economic output that places it in the top ten of nations, the California Endowment led by Dr. Robert Ross, a former Public Health Officer, and with Dr. Iton as Vice President, is investing one billion dollars in place-based initiatives, across fourteen communities state-wide, collectively referred to as *Building Health Communities*. Sharing a similar starting point with the social determinants of health, Dr. Kenneth W. Kizer is a founding director of the Institute for Population Health Improvement (IPHI), devoted to addressing challenges defined "as the overall health status or health outcomes of a specific group of people resulting from the many determinants of health, including health care, public health interventions, and social and environmental factors" with "population health management as taking purposeful actions to influence the health status or health outcomes..."(Institute for Population Health Improvement, 2015).

This is a book recounting the journeys in public health to address the social determinants of health and to improve population health. A professional biography of each of the authors is included. You will find the leadership work of Dr. Iton, Dr. Kizer and others in this book. The book looks to help you along that journey at whatever location you are in your career. The leadership lessons are from the inside out, drawing on experienced professionals in public health. The dual themes of inter-professionalism and the social determinants of health pervade the text and are a testament to the pressing need for emerging health professionals to become familiar with the expanding scope of public health and the range of stakeholders. The work is meant to complement rather than supplant existing primers or introductory books in public health by offering real-world case studies and cutting edge topics that will allow students and practitioners to bridge concepts and practice.

III. The Case Studies

No numbers without stories, no stories without numbers is a saying repeated by Dr. Bob Ross, who has led the California Endowment for the past ten years after serving as public health officer for the County and City of Philadelphia and the County of San Diego (Ross 2013). You will find numbers in this book and you will find stories. The stories focus on leadership practices that address the social determinants of health and advance population health. The utility of numbers is evident in this day of big data analytics (Bridgeland and Orzag 2013). Stories matter on a number of levels. From the perspective of leadership research, in the course of forty years of research and advising leaders in all sectors Warren Bennis (2009) has found effective storytelling to be an important leadership tool. As noted earlier, Marmot (2015) starts his most recent book with his story about himself as a young physician. Likewise, Iton has begun his presentations with his story as a Canadian witnessing the poverty of the City of Baltimore. In this book you will find that the personal narrative is a significant starting point for action.

From a research and teaching perspective, case studies allow for the use of case study methodology which provides an approach that explains the "how" of a complex issue (Yin 1994: 9). As the social determinants of health questions involve governance arrangements and decision-making processes, "...richly textured case studies" that are derived from field research can be more appropriate than other methods for developing a deep understanding of the complexities (Heinrich, Hill, and Lynn 2004: 13). The cases selected in this book draw on a wide range of perspectives from within foundations (the California Endowment and the Sierra Health Foundation) as catalysts for change, from major research universities (the University of California, Davis Medical Center, and the University of Southern California), and one of the two largest local public health departments (the Los Angeles County Department of Public Health). While the experiences are place-based, the leadership practices are developed in the cases and the concluding chapter to apply in other regions, to cross walk to other locations facing similar challenges in addressing the social determinants of health and improving population health.

IV. Transformational Leadership Practices

Each chapter shares a related starting point: the leadership does not accept the world as they find it. There is a recognition, driven by the data, that health outcomes and health inequities are entrenched, but also an underlying assumption that it does not have to be this way. This leadership assumption is foundational to leadership practices and research developed in the past fifty years since Burns' (1968) seminal work *On Leadership* introduced the distinction between transformational leadership, which fundamentally changes the roles and work, and transactional leadership, which focuses on exchanges between leaders and followers. This book draws on leadership practices that transform communities, organizations, and institutions to improve the lives of people and the health of populations. Each chapter recounts transformational leadership that literally transforms communities, neighborhoods, or organizations. The leadership practices in each chapter are not about maintaining the *status quo*. Rather, a starting point across each of the chapters is a questioning of the *status quo*. The first step in transformational leadership across each chapter is inquiry informed by data. The focus on transformational leadership does not diminish the role of strong management practices in public health; these are needed and essential for preventing disease, addressing outbreaks, responding to disasters, and the range of existing public management responsibilities. Rather, this contrast identifies that its core, addressing the social determinants of health and advancing population health, is a commitment to the transformation of individuals' health through transforming places—communities and neighborhoods, public health organizations, and ideas in public policy and health.

Recognizing the intensely cross-disciplinary nature of public health, as well as the various organizational designs for addressing public health, health care, and environmental health (Sinclair and Whitford 2012), this book draws on a wide range of leadership lessons that start with a deep recognition of the complexities of the social determinants of health, and the varied leadership practices needed to address the complexities of these issues. The complexities are both vertical and horizontal in working with others. There is an ongoing need to navigate and negotiate the intergovernmental system of federal, state, county, and local government relations. The horizontal challenges include working across sectors, public, nonprofit, and for profit, as well as the prominence of philanthropy as a fourth sector. The complexities include the challenges of both scaling up good ideas, proven to work in one jurisdiction, and cross-walking them to another location, as well as the challenges of discovering new ways to address seemingly intractable challenges at the core of the social determinants of health. Other features adding to the complexities are information uncertainties in a turbulent environment. The leadership practices described in this book start with inquiry because the complexities have not been solved through conventional thinking.

The urgency, complexities, and consequences of leadership addressing the social determinants of health complexities are captured well in a framework developed by Don Kettle to explain "... wicked problems that defy our organizational and policy boundaries, these past models provide a poor guide for future action" (Kettle 2006: 276–281). Kettle finds five features categorize these wicked problems:

- Looking back instead of looking forward
- Reforming instead of governing
- Thinking vertically instead of horizontally
- Regulating instead of performing
- A misplaced veneration for outdated traditions instead of a focus on effective governance

The emerging practices outlined in this book respond to each of these features. Moreover, the cases and examples in this book, the leadership thinking and practices respond to the need to replenish depleted intellectual capital in facing the new challenges of each disaster. The past approaches do not adequately address the scope and scale of problems identified in current thinking on the social determinants of health and population health. Rather than relying on past models, this book draws on new examples to generate new intellectual capital needed to get traction on addressing the underlying social issues impeding individual and community health.

The transformational focus of each chapter does not present an orthodoxy to be embraced. Instead, the diversity of approaches invites the readers to consider the leadership practices as catalyst for thinking about adaptation in their local communities. Public health is indeed a manifestation of local issues that are affected by a myriad of stakeholders and decision-makers at different levels of governance. Among the challenges for the next generation of leaders will be addressing the need for, and development of, innovative models of interprofessional training, collaboration, and service delivery. Moving from assessment to action is a central theme of this book and is woven throughout the chapters to illustrate the possibilities for innovation to secure population health, particularly among vulnerable populations.

The metaphor that expresses the goals of the book is of adding a variety of tools to your existing toolbox, building on your existing skill set. New tools, new concepts facilitate transformational practices and new strategies to address seemingly intractable and long-standing inequities.

This book is premised on the concept that a variety of tools and perspectives are needed to address the complexities of place-based challenges inherent in addressing the social determinants of health, and population health improvements will find great variety in adaptation of the practices discussed in this book. Similar to the thirty years of research recognized with the Nobel Prize in 2009 to Elinor Ostrom (2010) aimed at protecting common pool resources in the environment, the cross-disciplinary and cross-cultural responses to social determinants of health and population health will have varied local adaptation in communities, organizations, and institutions, but will share similar principles and solve similar challenges.

V. Outline of the Book

This is a book for professionals and aspiring professionals in public management, public health, and related programs that provide theoretical frameworks coupled with actionable, practical insights into cutting-edge topics in public health and healthcare. This approach is founded on the premise that there is no single approach but rather a set of leadership practices that draws from a diverse array of professional skills. The work illustrates the complexity of contemporary issues at the intersection of public health and healthcare and the compelling need to engage numerous public and private stakeholders to effectively advance population health.

The work is divided into three parts that focus on the new role of public health departments, emerging challenges and opportunities following the enactment of the Patient Protection and Affordable Care Act (ACA), and recent trends in innovation and investment. Each chapter is practice-oriented to provide insight into the changing landscape of public health while offering practical tips based on the experiences and expertise of leading practitioners. The first section, Public Health Departments: Scope, Systems, and Standards, continues from this chapter, with the second chapter focused on the Modernization of Public Health Departments and written by Jonathan Freedman, who draws on a twenty-five-year career in healthcare systems and public health for the County of Los Angeles, serving over ten million residents. Freedman's final posting in the department was as Chief Deputy, directing operations of the second largest public health department in the United States. The third chapter discusses Accreditation and Credentialing, in which Dru Bhattacharya draws on his experience as a public health practitioner, researcher, and current Chair and Director of a Master of Public Health degree program with a deep understanding of the process and value of accrediting public health programs, and the pressing challenges in education, training, and practice. This chapter critically examines the current landscape of accreditation and credentialing by focusing on standards promulgated by the Public Health Accreditation Board to accredit public health departments; the Council on Education for Public Health and its accreditation of public health programs; and the National Board of Public Health Examiners and its 'Certified in Public Health' credential.

The second part of the book is organized around Post-Affordable Care Act Challenges and Opportunities. This section looks at the changing landscape of healthcare, driven by the passage of the Affordable Care Act (ACA), starting with the fourth chapter of the book that explores novel interprofessional collaborations. Written by Dru Bhattacharya, this chapter highlights the development of, and opportunity for, medical-legal partnerships to advance population health. Drawing from original research and surveys, this chapter explores the utilization of the MLP as a locus of research and intervention, and identifies precisely how to establish meaningful collaboration among legal and healthcare practitioners to advance population health. The fifth chapter builds upon the knowledge and insights gleaned from novel partnerships and related assessments, but focuses on formulating decisions within strategic environments. Written by Dru Bhattacharya and Dr. Jay Bhatt, this chapter utilizes a game theoretic-epidemiological model within a medical-legal partnership to analyze strategic interaction and advance population health. Moving beyond traditional economic models of evaluation, the emphasis on strategic thinking and decision making highlights the upstream opportunities to advance health by incorporating tools that have been historically rooted in managerial economics and business strategy.

The third section of the book is the core of the focus on Innovation and Investment, addressing the social determinants of health. The sixth chapter introduces the importance of place-based analysis with Understanding How Health Happens: Your Zip Code Is More Important Than Your Genetic Code. Written by the Vice President for Building Healthy Communities in the California Endowment, Dr. Anthony Iton, and the President and Chief Executive Officer of the California Endowment, Dr. Robert Ross, this chapter draws on their careers as public health officers on the east coast and west coast, in urban areas, as well as their current efforts nearly mid-way through a ten-year, $1 billion tranche of funding for place-based initiatives in California. The seventh chapter continues the focus on place-based change to address the social determinants of health through Designing Partnerships and Building Relationships. Written by Chet Hewitt, President and CEO of Sierra Health Foundation, the chapter draws on Hewitt's current efforts and his career in philanthropy, as well as in Alameda County directing the Children's Protective Services and then the Human Services Agency. The eighth chapter explores funding innovations with a focus on Social Impact Bonds: Legal and Leadership Considerations by Dru Bhattacharya. The ninth chapter describes the founding of the Institute for Population Health Improvement at a major medical research center, UC Davis, and the emergence of partnerships with Improving Population Health through Clinical–Community Collaboration. The chapter draws on Dr. Kenneth W. Kizer's current experience as founding director of IPHI, as well as his healthcare career that included leading the largest vertically integrated healthcare system in the United States, as Undersecretary for the Veterans' Health Administration. The section concludes with the tenth chapter describing a successful community-based effort aimed at Addressing Health Inequities written by Lavonna Blair Lewis, a cutting-edge researcher who successfully partners with communities to deepen the understanding of underserved community needs, as well as a well-respected teacher and a past director of graduate programs in health.

The final section of the book, in chapter eleven, highlights the themes that emerge as the Leadership Practices found throughout this book.

Written by Richard Callahan, the chapter draws on his insights from the chapters and discussions with the authors, as well as his past fifteen years of experience in developing, designing, and delivering leadership programs internationally, nationally, statewide, regionally, and locally, across the public and nonprofit sectors.

As you work through a chapter, an important leadership practice is to step off the dance floor and look down from the balcony. To extend the metaphor, in each chapter there is the action on the dance floor—the sequence of events in each chapter, the locations, and the programs. Stepping to the balcony invites you to see the leadership practices that initiated those events, focused on the locations, and started programs. The perspective from the balcony offers insights into the actions that bring the partners together, and that provide direction to the activity. The perspective above the dance floor allows us to ask what core values motivate the actions, how these values are advanced in the activity, and what all the motions add up to when seen collectively. The balcony invites you to see the "what and how" of these efforts to address the social determinants of health. Also, as you read the chapter, stepping back and stepping onto the balcony allows you to ask what lessons, insights, and leadership practices you can adapt to the specifics of your circumstances, to expand public health and other fields in a coordinated and designed set of efforts to address the social determinants of health.

VI. Outcomes

There are several outcomes this book intends to generate for the reader. The first of these is leadership practices that help you get traction on needed change. These practices will include examples of gathering and applying data, developing strategy, identifying funding, and engaging partners. The second is examples and data that will deepen your understanding of the social determinants of health and population health. These examples draw from a range of locations and sectors. The third aim is to improve your abilities to find leverage points for change. This will include examples of leverage points in existing public health systems, as well as in the intergovernmental system and in partnerships with philanthropy. The fourth is to provide practices for identifying population health needs. These practices will include data gathering, partnering with public agencies, and development of recommendations. Finally, the book aims to facilitate a reduced reliance on the direct delivery of clinical services with suggestions for improved leveraging of existing resources.

The insights in each chapter draw on leadership practices that are currently working. These are not aspirational practices, in the sense that we would like health leaders to do the following. Rather, these are evidence-based practices, that have been shown to work in complex, challenging circumstances. Leadership may be easy to talk about—or, as noted by the president of a large research university, everyone wants to be president of a university, but few want to do the actual work of a university president (Sample, 2003). The chapters are intended to help you develop transformational programs, adapting lessons from the chapters to address the social determinants of health and advance population health in the communities, regions, and states that you serve.

References

Bennis, W. with P. W. Biederman. 2009. The leader as storyteller. *The Essential Bennis*. San Francisco, CA: Jossey-Bass.

Bridgeland. J. and P. Orzag. 2013. Can government play moneyball? How a new era of scarcity can make Washington work better. *The Atlantic*. July. http://www.theatlantic.com/**magazine**/archive/2013/07/can-government-play-moneyball/309389/. Accessed April 20, 2016.

Burns, J. M. 1978. *On Leadership*. New York: Harper & Row Publishers, Inc.

Edelman, M. (producer). 2011. *The Passion and Politics of Ed Edelman*, http://video.pbssocal.org/program/passion-and-politics-ed-edelman/

Gladwell, M. 2015. Starting over: many Katrina victims left New Orleans for good. What can we learn from them? *The New Yorker*. August 24.

Harlem Children's Zone. 2015. *A community of opportunity: 2014–2015 biennial report*. http://wac.adef.edgecastcdn.net/80ADEF/hcz.org/wp-content/uploads/2015/11/HCZ-Biennial-Report-2014-2015-single-pages.pdf. Accessed 20 April, 2016.

Heinrich, C. J., C. Hill and L. E. Lynn, Jr. 2004. Governance as an organizing theme for empirical research. *Art of Governance: Analyzing Management and Administration*. Ed. P. W. Ingraham and L. E. Lynn, Jr. 3–19. Washington, D.C.: Georgetown University Press.

Institute for Population Health Improvement. http://www.ucdmc.ucdavis.edu/iphi/abouttemp.html

Iton, A. 2015. Building Health Communities: Interview with Tony Iton (Part 1). http://www.whatworksforamerica.org/building-health-communities-interview-with-tony-iton-part-1/#.VxgVtL59Jbx. Accessed 20 April, 2016.

Kettle, D. F. 2006. Is the worst yet to come? *Annals of the American Academy of Political and Social Science*. 604(1): 273–287.

Kirlin, J. 1996. What government must do well: creating value for society. *Journal of Public Administration Research and Theory*. 6: 161–185.

Marmot, M. 2015. *The Health Gap: The Challenge of an Unequal World*. London: Bloomsbury.

Marmot, M. and J.J. Allen. 2014, Social Determinants of Health Equity. *American Journal of Public Health Editorial*. 104S: S4–S519.

Ostrom, E. 2010. Beyond markets and states: polycentric governance of complex economic systems. *American Economic Review*. 100: 641–672.

Ross, R. 2013. Building Healthy Communities: Change the World From Here. Lecture, University of San Francisco. 2013. http://tinyurl.com/puus5wk

Sample, S. 2003. *The Contrarian's Guide to Leadership*. CA. San Francisco: Jossey-Bass Publishers.

Sinclair, A.H. and A. B. Whitford. 2012. Separation and integration in public health: evidence from organizational structure in the States. *Journal of Public Administration Research and Theory*. 23: 55–77.

Yin, R. K. 1994. *Case Study Research: Designs and Methods*. Second edition. Thousand Oaks, CA: Sage Publications.

2 Building a High Performing Public Health Department

Leadership through Navigating and Negotiating

Jonathan Freedman, MSPH

I. Introduction

This chapter offers insights for leadership in public health drawn from over twenty years of professional experience serving a county of ten million residents, on the adaptation needed by public health departments in the United States to address health issues in the twenty-first century.

Public health departments confront unprecedented challenges and opportunities. Public health leaders face growing expectations of public health agencies involved in land use planning and transportation, not just from the perspective of environmental regulation and injury control, but in relation to quality of life issues like access to parks and the availability of walking and bike paths. Challenges are broad and range from improving internal performance, including training staff in dual functions for emergencies, as well as coping with cyclic and reactive public health funding streams, to addressing new, persistent, and re-emerging public health issues and threats in the context of population growth, globalization, and the federal Affordable Care Act (ACA). The opportunities are large for public health as public attitudes, and the views of public policy-makers and opinion-leaders—primarily through the lens of the ACA—are pushing for action on health issues such as healthy eating and active living that are influenced by factors well beyond the scope of the healthcare sector and the expansion of national health insurance. Globalization, climate change, and the ACA are imperatives that demand public health departments to examine, improve, and re-tool their role in addressing population health.

Globalization and climate change force public health departments to review and adapt plans because the very nature of these concerns means they have worldwide dimensions that play out at local levels. Globalization challenges mean that local public health and healthcare infrastructures need to be prepared for new health threats because U.S. cities and the health concerns of the developing world are just a plane ride apart. Local public health effects of climate change mean that public health departments need to be prepared for extreme weather and changing housing and transportation patterns.

The health insurance expansion under the ACA, the most sweeping health law of the last hundred years, shapes the way in which public health departments have historically provided clinical services that serve both public health and safety net healthcare objectives. Persons with ACA coverage have less reliance on safety net services. Like many elements of the U.S. health sector, the ACA challenges institutions and structures established pre-ACA to adapt to be both responsive to the needs of the previously uninsured and accommodate the requirements of the ACA (Boutwell and Freedman 2014).

II. Public Health Departments

First, some level-setting for the reader about the usage of the term *public health department*. Public health departments, or what can be called governmental public health, form a subset of the larger field of public health. The larger public health field has many definitions (American Public Health Association; World Health Organization) and is carried out by many individuals and entities, globally and locally, in both governmental and non-governmental sectors. I use my own simple definition: public health is the combination of social justice and science to identify and improve the conditions which impact population health, and governmental public health is those actions organized, funded, administered, and carried out by public health departments in which specific legal authorities (i.e. health officer powers, regulatory powers, police powers) have been granted. Thus, public health departments are components of a larger field, and governmental public health entities carry out specific functions.

An important starting point is to understand that there is no national public health system in the United States. There is a system of state, local, and federal public health agencies operating independently and (on occasion) in coordination with other each other. A reference to public health department means a state, local, or regional entity and not the federal Centers for Disease Control and Prevention (CDC). State, local, and regional public health departments perform the bulk of public health activities in the United States with support and guidance, and in limited instances directives, from CDC. This is a federal system, decentralized throughout the United States. My experience suggests that we do not have a national system of public health. Rather, there is a system of state, local, and federal public health agencies nationally.

III. Essentials for Today

Public health practitioners in the U.S. face large challenges just accomplishing daily activities, let alone preparing for and adapting to new challenges. In communities throughout the U.S. each day, public health departments face important issues such as the interruption of potable water sources, illness clusters in childcare centers or schools, or infection control problems in hospitals or other institutions. Public health departments also have to address the forces of elected officials and their governing bodies, and "reactive" funding cycles— elected officials who demand action on a particular public health concern, provide targeted resources, and want results and accountability for the investment of public resources.

Because public health is a field and not a discipline, identifying and maintaining the skill base and systems for core functions cannot be underestimated. For example, the skill base of the workforce needed to carry out the "basic six" functions of a public health department identified over sixty years ago (Emerson and Luginbuhl 1945) is immense. The basic six are:

- vital statistics (birth, death, and morbidity records)
- laboratory services
- health education
- maternal and child health
- communicable disease control
- environmental health

These functions require highly trained physicians, sanitarians, nurses, epidemiologists, statisticians, and laboratorians, to name a few. Of course, up to date equipment, resources, and information technology is essential for this work.

"Nothing happens" is the adage used by experienced public health professionals when public health departments function well and do their job. There is no reporting or press release of the disease outbreak that did not happen because of effective environmental regulation, disease reporting, contact investigation and intervention. However, when public health departments break down, often because of a lack of appropriate skills and resources, the results can be large and widespread—delayed investigation, a continuing health threat, illness and death, and loss of public confidence. It is the job of the public health leader—the public manager—to acquire, align, and maintain the readiness of the skills and technology to keep ongoing disease risks in check and rapidly respond to emergent threats.

IV. Moving Beyond Daily Demands

Keeping pace with the above daily demands is not the limit of the full job in today's public health department. A new nimbleness is required, calling for a skill set to navigate and negotiate in a challenging terrain. The toolbox for the public health leader must include an internal examination of public health department operations, and an external assessment of the needed partners in the community to leverage work.

Public health departments are being asked to pay greater attention to public health emergency responses, and tackle new burdens in human health such as obesity, physical activity, and behavioral health (Trust for America's Health 2013). For the most part emergency response can be built upon the core public health functions with some adjustments (Callahan, Clayton, and Haverty 2008), while chronic disease intervention often requires new investments and skills. Both the old and the new public health require the formulation of inter-sector partnerships with law and fire agencies, schools, the media, the healthcare community, and others.

The first key step in identifying the appropriate pathway to modernize and adapt current functions and reach into new public health areas can be difficult. Fortunately, there are a number of ways to approach this work. A simple approach might be to clearly identify what has been assigned to your department in terms of legal mandates and obligations, what health assessment work is occurring in terms of traditional morbidity and mortality, and identify which gaps need to be filled. This can be accomplished via a traditional annual budget process or a more formal public health planning process that establishes community health goals. In this area, the national Healthy People 2020 (www.healthypeople.gov) is an important document to align planning toward national health goals. The Community Guide (www.thecommunityguide.org) developed by the national Community Preventive Services Task Force is a powerful tool which provides guidance on effective preventive health interventions at the community level.

A second leadership practice is to leverage the accreditation process. The movement to strengthen public health departments has been greatly assisted by the efforts to develop the accreditation of public health departments. While participation is voluntary, the Public Health Accreditation Board (PHAB) (www.phaboard.org) and its accreditation process is the most advanced tool to systematically examine and improve public health department performance. The PHAB process is not only an internal performance improvement program, but is also specifically tied to a Community Health Assessment Plan and a Community Health Improvement Plan.

V. Data Driving Leadership Practices

There is perhaps no more significant role for public health than the regular assessment and reporting of community health. Morbidity and mortality assessments largely derived by birth and death records, and communicable disease reporting, are central to this endeavor. Timely production of reporting is essential to identify trends, and this needs to be coupled with careful interpretation to inform the community, and implement and/or adapt interventions.

Surveillance for chronic disease, physical activity, and social and environmental determinants of health is a core competency of a modern public health department. There are many approaches to this work such as measurement of the healthcare system, community health surveys, and household interview surveys.

Improving the traditional health assessment apparatus of measuring death and "bugs and germs" is important to do, along with building new health measurement systems. Many health departments, such as in Los Angeles County, have made large investments in health assessment to modernize traditional morbidity and mortality and improve timeliness. For the Los Angeles County Department of Public Health (LACDPH), this has been accomplished by the automation of birth and death records from hospitals and the funeral industry, and the deployment of electronic reporting for more than fifty communicable diseases by large segments of the healthcare industry, particularly hospitals and laboratories. Electronic reporting has reduced the cycle time to generate health assessment reports, as well as shortened the response time for communicable disease intervention such as contact tracing.

Los Angeles County, like many other jurisdictions, has deployed a household interview survey which queries residents on health conditions, health behaviors, and demographics. Many of the survey questions tie to state and national surveys like the federal American Community Survey so that local results can be compared to state and national figures (Fielding, Teutsch, and Caldwell 2013).

But most importantly, combining old and new health assessment capability has created new ways to look at disease burden in the population. As framed by McGuiness and Foege in 1993, traditional health statistics measure death and disease, but other data is needed to demonstrate their underlying factors (see also http://www.ncbi.nlm.nih.gov/pubmed/8411605). Thus, the public health practitioner is not simply measuring and reporting the number of cancer or vehicular deaths in a community, but is also able to tie mortality to underlying causes such as tobacco usage and air quality or alcohol consumption, respectively. This type of health assessment also allows the public health department to examine leading causes of premature death from chronic disease and injury along with communicable disease.

VI. Changing the Planning Horizon

Leaders combining the use of traditional and new health assessment tools can change the planning horizon from core functions and the "basic six" to involvement in many sectors and domains beyond the health sector. For example, because of modern health assessment approaches tobacco control has shifted away from interventions at the individual level (i.e. cessation) to the policy level in domains outside of health, such as tobacco taxation and the environmental regulation of tobacco use in public places. Similarly, approaches to healthy eating and active living are focused on domains traditionally far from the field of public health. Now, public health agencies have found themselves intimately involved with land use planning and transportation not just from the perspective of environmental regulation and injury control, but also in relation to quality of life issues like access to parks and the availability of walking and bike paths.

The public health improvement work complements the work of the public health leader in the engagement partners externally. The ability of public health to define a community problem in terms of data and impact, in terms of cause and effect, and in terms of roles and responsibilities are powerful tools to bring partners together. For example, in Los Angeles County public health leaders were able to demonstrate the impact of sedentary behaviors that impact community health. This work led to engagement with the metropolitan transportation planning agency to promote walking and biking in the Los Angeles area transportation plan, which prioritizes road and highway funding. In doing this work, public health needed to be aware of the challenges facing their partners. Also, in this case public health needed to understand the regional and political forces affecting the transportation agency, and needed to familiarize itself with its policy and funding cycles in order to find the best way to partner so that public health was not simply prescribing a responsibility to a partner with no interest or capability in implementation. Optimally, inter-sector partnerships are in areas that are mutually beneficial or mission critical to each partner, so that each party is motivated toward the common goal.

VII. Workforce Competencies and Skill Mix

The workforce competencies and skill mix needed to run an effective twenty-first century public health department are significant. Traditional public health workers—physicians, nurses, epidemiologists, sanitarians, statisticians, health educators, and laboratorians—must be present and operating at maximal levels. Furthermore, because of the new health assessment models and emerging roles of public health outside of its historic domains, new skills are needed. Such is the case in Los Angeles County, in which new competencies were added to the workforce including economists, sociologists, lawyers, and urban planners. Additionally, finding staff with the sophistication to engage in cross-sector partnerships is essential, requiring experience in public affairs, communications, and public policy.

In Los Angeles County, the modernized public health workforce was developed in the following manner. All current and new staff were trained on the core functions of the department. Initial training included four to eight hours of internal training on core public health practice and new health assessment tools, and all workers were trained as disaster service workers to establish a posture that all public health workers are potentially "first responders" in emergency incidents. More specific training followed, tied closely to the worker's role and the science base and operational requirements of their assigned program area. Further, staff who may be needed in a larger scale public health emergency response were additionally trained. Thus, the modern public health department had this mix of staff: highly trained professionals for traditional and core functions; newer staff and skills to address new and emerging public health challenges of chronic disease; and all staff trained for large scale emergency response.

In 2010, the impact of developing this skill mix became evident when the LACDPH, with its 4,000 staff, was able to provide more than 240,000 vaccinations in roughly 45 days during the H1N1 influenza response, and maintain essential public health functions during the same time frame. This was accomplished by continuity of operations planning, in which there was a pre-determination of the public health functions that could be "turned-off" in an emergency, and which staff could be redeployed into emergency response. Redeployable staff were cross-trained in emergency response competencies and roles. For example, maternal and child health, sexually transmitted disease, and chronic disease functions were identified in advance as services that could be reduced or halted in an emergency, and those workers were trained in emergency response. The development of "dual use" staff was critical in creating a supply of licensed and clinically trained personnel needed as vaccinators in a response like H1N1. Dual use staff were provided with both periodic emergency response training, as well as just-in-time training such as "brush-up" training on vaccine administration. Because of this planning and training, Los Angeles County was able to shift more than 1,000 dual use staff into the H1N1 response, who supplemented and backed up the 1,000 core staff already deployed.

VIII. Coordination and Partnerships

Because public health is a field and not a discipline, public health professionals have historically had to develop partnerships both internally and externally. The demand for internal coordination and alignment in a public health department and across its varied professionals is large, sometimes difficult, and can be a full time job. However, public health cannot limit itself to organizing its internal operations because much of public health, and almost all of the new demands of public health, occur via sectors outside of the public health department.

Take, for example, the public health challenge of substance abuse. Internal to a public health department, substance abuse prevention and control touches on the different ways departments have been historically organized—populations (i.e. maternal and child health), diseases and risk factors (i.e. STDs, TB and other communicable diseases), and geographies (i.e. public health field operations). For a public health department, determining where to anchor a function organizationally and how to implement program interventions across the internal "silos" can be a large challenge. Regrettably, because much of public health funding is reactive, based on responses to public problems or constituency-driven causes, silos in public health departments are significant. Consequently, silos based on funding streams tend to dominate the organizational structure of many public health departments.

Two tools combat this phenomena: one, public health leaders must advocate to their policy makers that investment in a core program that is flexible to respond to a wide variety of threats is essential. Second, the public health leader must, as a manager, consistently reinforce the internal inter-dependence of public health activities. The communicable disease risk of blood-borne pathogens provides a good example. Many public health departments look at hepatitis prevention and response in a siloed manner, often seeing it separately as a behavioral risk factor, an occupational hazard, and a communicable disease threat.

Regardless of organization and funding rules, effective public health leaders must develop the internal partnerships so that energy can be focused across internal barriers. Joint planning can delineate functional roles and responsibilities tied to the input and output metrics needed to deliver community public health objectives. The value of the PHAB process mentioned above is that it shifts the focus of public health department work from activities and projects occurring in silos into a comprehensive effort. This effort across silos can target goals delineated in a Community Health Improvement Plan that is driven by a Community Health Assessment.

The effective public health leader leverages the demands of modernization and funding rules to blend efforts. In Los Angeles County, three strategies help to move in this direction. The first was the development of emergency response planning that focused on all hazards rather than each specific or individual incident. The second was the identification and control of all discretionary funding sources to be used in a flexible form to fund activities that could not be funded by other sources. The third was greater control of siloed funding streams, so that they could be aligned and transformed into a component of a larger overall public health model.

However, far more exciting than the internal machinations of a public health department are the external partnerships that need to be formed. Because the footprint of modern public health well exceeds the footprint of a public health department, gaining the engagement of new sectors is critical. Los Angeles County has made significant investments in external partnerships, some of which are circumstantial while others were strategic. The H1N1 example demonstrates both the circumstantial and the strategic.

The circumstantial partnerships for Los Angeles County public health are driven by the reality that Los Angeles County has no metropolitan government. Although the County is the largest local government entity, there are 88 cities and 82 school districts, and emergency response roles are distributed across each of these entities. While the County health officer retains command authority in health threat response, the actual implementation often occurs via inter-agency work. Thus, in the H1N1 response, community vaccinations typically occurred in public parks and schools operated by other governmental entities. Large investments were made by the County and its governmental partners in pre-incident planning and exercises that tested and refined these partnerships before use. For example, plans to identify community sites for mass vaccination were tested during the public health department's annual influenza vaccination campaign.

The H1N1 response benefited from strategic partnerships developed for other public health initiatives. For example, partnerships with the Chamber of Commerce primarily focused on promoting the value of employee wellness proved invaluable to public health because of the need to communicate with the business community about the facts and myths of H1N1. Similarly, the partnerships developed with schools aimed at making school athletic fields available to the community as park space cleared the way for discussions on how to use school sites as community vaccination centers.

Strategic partnerships take time to develop and likely cannot be durable and usable unless each party understands and accepts, at least to some degree, the demands and limitations of the other. Los Angeles County's involvement in bioterrorism threat assessment and response in partnership with the Los Angeles District Office of the Federal Bureau of Investigation (FBI) provides a good example. LACDPH and the FBI developed a partnership for joint investigation of intelligence bioterrorism incidents. This partnership established the roles and responsibilities of public health staff and FBI agents, and delineated the way in which agency staff can jointly investigate cases. This was not an easy partnership as public health was concerned about the risk to public trust and cooperation if it was viewed as an arm of law enforcement, while the FBI wanted to maintain control and custody of an investigation. A joint exercise, performed in real time with over 100 combined staff, helped to work out the kinks and test the concept. It involved joint interviews of suspects and victims (actually played by theatrical actors), and the transfer of information between agencies in a secure manner. Through this, the FBI learned where public health needed to maintain patient confidentiality in order to elicit trust, and the public health learned that it can assist law enforcement with the interpretation of data and information without undermining public trust.

IX. Conclusion

In the twenty-first century, public health departments are tasked with improving their core performance, while simultaneously expanding their central role in larger community health issues often defined by demographics, genetics, behaviors, society, and the environment. Both performance improvement and the new roles require public health departments—particularly their leaders, administrators, and managers—to look critically at their operations. Internal and external partnerships also play a key role modernizing public health, whether it is aligning siloed programs or establishing new relationships with sectors previously far afield. There are many ways to undertake improvement efforts, including internal assessments, audits, and professional reviews, or more formal new tools such as PHAB accreditation. The key starting point is to recognize the role of leadership in identifying the existing and emerging terrain, navigating those areas, negotiating partnerships, and testing in advance of crisis.

References

American Public Health Association—https://www.apha.org/about-apha

Boutwell, A. E. and J. Freedman. 2014. Coverage expansion and the criminal justice-involved population: Implications for plans and service connectivity. *Health Affairs*, 33(3): 482–486. doi: 10.1377/hlthaff.2013.1131

Callahan, T., R. Clayton, and D. Haverty 2008. *Preparing for Disasters*, Washington, DC: The IBM Center for The Business of Government. http://www.businessofgovernment.org/sites/default/files/PreparingDisatersBrief.pdf

Community Preventive Services Task Force, Community Guide. www.thecommunityguide.org

Emerson H. and M. Luginbuhl. 1945. *Local Health Units for the Nation.* American Public Health Association Committee on Administrative Practice, Subcommittee on Local Health Units. The Commonwealth Fund.

Fielding J.E., S.M. Teutsch, and S.N. Caldwell (eds.). 2013. *Public Health Practice: What Works.* Oxford: Oxford University Press.

Healthy People 2020. www.healthypeople.gov

McGinnis, J. M. and W.H. Foege. 1993. Actual causes of death in the United States. *Journal of the American Medical Association* 70(18): 2207–2212.

Public Health Accreditation Board. phaboard.org

Trust for America's Health. 2013. "Foundational" Capabilities of Public Health Departments, January: http://healthyamericans.org/health-issues/wp-content/uploads/2014/03/Kuehnert_FoundationalCap_22814.pdf

World Health Organization—Constitution and Bylaws. Basic Documents, 48th Edition, http://apps.who.int/gb/bd/PDF/bd48/basic-documents-48th-edition-en.pdf#page=7

3 Accreditation and Credentialing

Pressing Challenges in Education, Training, and Practice

Dru Bhattacharya, JD, MPH, LLM

I. Introduction

As the Chair of a Department of Population Health Sciences, Director of a public health program, and mentor for over one hundred students in a given year, I am concerned about the current landscape of accreditation and credentialing as it relates to education, training, and practice. There is a clear disconnect among educators, students, and employers as to the precise skills and competencies that ought to be developed (and when). Against a backdrop of shortages in our public health workforce, a broader discussion on the current standards of accreditation and credentialing as they relate to education and training is timely and imperative.

At the outset, we ought to recognize that there is no singular definition or characteristic of a public health professional. Candidates leverage a formal degree or advanced training in public health at different times in their career trajectory for very different purposes. Traditional candidates include aspiring or current practitioners in medicine, nursing, and other allied health professions. Others are simply eager to take a non-healthcare associated pathway to improve health and well-being among populations, and still others are perhaps mid-career or seasoned professionals who are eager to switch careers, or perhaps further develop critical competencies for advancement within their own organization, respectively. Their contributions are equally diverse, encompassing roles and responsibilities in leadership, management and administration, research, education, advocacy, and healthcare delivery—all part of a broader spectrum of the essential services that together constitute "public health". This diversity is a testament to health being recognized as a social construct, requiring multiple actors and factors to align for its assurance and realization. At the same time, it poses a remarkable challenge in articulating the precise skills and competencies that we ought to inculcate in our formal training and education, historically at the graduate level and now also at the undergraduate level, as well as continuing and executive education among professionals.

In this chapter, we explore the current landscape of accreditation and credentialing by focusing on standards promulgated by the Public Health Accreditation Board to accredit public health departments; the Council on Education for Public Health and its accreditation of public health programs; and the National Board of Public Health Examiners and its 'Certified in Public Health' credential. We shall not scrutinize these instruments in isolation, but rather inquire as to how well they are currently aligned with one another with respect to the general expectations of public health professionals. This practice-oriented approach begins with the specific standards proffered by the Public Health Accreditation Board, followed by a reflection on the current (and revised) accreditation standards of the Council on Education for Public Health and the National Board of Public Health Examiners.

II. Public Health Accreditation Board

The Public Health Accreditation Board (PHAB) is a non-profit organization that affords voluntary national accreditation to health departments to improve service, value, and accountability to stakeholders. As of 2016 over 117 health departments were accredited, with 181 departments with applications in progress. Eligibility is open to a governmental entity that has the primary statutory or legal responsibility for public health in a Tribe, state, territory, or at the local level. According to the National Association of County and City Health Organizations, there are over 2,800 local health departments in the U.S. Along with 50 states, and approximately 198 tribal health departments, this would amount to an estimated total of 3,048 health departments eligible for accreditation. At present, less than 4% of eligible health departments have been accredited, and even accounting for the successful accreditation of those applications in progress, this would increase to under 10% of eligible departments.

The PHAB has developed twelve domains and attendant standards within each domain within its most recent document, Standards and Measures Version 1.5, which provides guidance for departments preparing for accreditation. The domains are summarized below, and also appear along with the attendant standards in Appendix 1.

1   **Assess**—Conduct and disseminate assessments focused on population health status and public health issues facing the community.
2   **Investigate**—Investigate health problems and environmental public health hazards to protect the community.
3   **Inform and Educate**—Inform and educate about public health issues and functions.
4   **Community Engagement**—Engage with the community to identify and address health problems.
5   **Policies and Plans**—Develop public health policies and plans.

6 **Public Health Laws**—Enforce public health laws.
7 **Access to Care**—Promote strategies to promote access to health care.
8 **Workforce**—Maintain a competent public health workforce.
9 **Quality Improvement**—Evaluate and continuously improve processes, programs, and interventions.
10 **Evidence**—Contribute to and apply the evidence base of public health.
11 **Administration and Management**—Maintain administrative and management capacity.
12 **Governance**—Maintain capacity to engage the public health governing entity.

If public health departments are expected to execute their functions across these domains, it is only fitting that candidates seeking advanced training in public health should be adept at performing basic tasks and functions consistent with these responsibilities. The Council on Education for Public Health (CEPH) oversees compliance with the accreditation standards of public health education. This is an independent agency recognized by the U.S. Department of Education to accredit schools and programs in public health. A cursory review of these domains alongside the current accreditation standards of the Council on Education for Public Health (CEPH) suggests consistency across the domains. At present, the CEPH program accreditation standards (effective June 2011 to present) provide that all graduate professional public health degree programs afford sufficient "Public Health Core Knowledge" in five core areas of public health, including biostatistics, epidemiology, environmental health sciences, health services administration, and social and behavioral sciences. We might align the PHAB domains with these areas of public health core knowledge in Table 3.1.

Notwithstanding the general alignment of domains with core areas of knowledge, there are some notable gaps, particularly in the absence of required knowledge as relates to public health law, the workforce, and governance. This is problematic considering that the public health law is neither required nor necessarily included in a core course on health services administration. In fact, in most public health programs it is offered as an elective and invariably populated by students concentrating in health policy and management.

Yet even within the general domains where we may observe some overlap with the CEPH criteria, the attendant standards illustrate potential gaps in the core areas of knowledge. Consider Domain 1 and the presumed alignment with biostatistics and epidemiology.

Table 3.1 General Alignment of PHAB Domains with CEPH Core Knowledge

PHAB Domain	CEPH Core Knowledge
1. Assess	Biostatistics, Epidemiology, Social/Behavioral
2. Investigate	Epidemiology, Environmental
3. Inform and Educate	Social/Behavioral
4. Community Engagement	Social/Behavioral
5. Policies and Plan	Health Services Admin
6. Public Health Laws	–
7. Access to Care	Biostatistics, Epidemiology, Health Services Admin
8. Workforce	–
9. Quality Improvement	Health Services Admin
10. Evidence-based Practices	Biostatistics, Epidemiology, Social/Behavioral
11. Administration and Management	Health Services Admin
12. Governance	–

Table 3.2 Highlighting Potential Disconnect between Standards and Core Knowledge

Domain 1, "Assess" PHAB		CEPH (2011)
Standard 1.1	Participate in or lead a collaborative process resulting in a comprehensive Community Health Assessment.	–
Standard 1.3	Analyze public health data to identify trends in health problems...	Biostatistics, Epidemiology

Here, we find that the core knowledge afforded by biostatistics and epidemiology would adequately meet Standard 1.3 as relates to analyzing public health data to identify trends in health problems. At the same time, there is no clear alignment with the competency to effectively craft a Community Health Assessment. To be sure, a graduate student in public health may be able to quickly grasp the essential requirements of, and undertake the tasks for, conducting such an assessment. Still, given that the complexities of such an assessment are driven by factors unique to the communities within which it is conducted, and the relationships forged in the process of acquiring this information, there is no substitute for the experience and insight acquired from *doing* the assessment.

The proposed revisions to the CEPH accreditation standards have essentially done away with the notion of core areas unique to essentially five traditional disciplines of public health, and have now focused on knowledge as it relates to thirteen broad learning objectives falling within the two categories of the "Profession and Science of Public Health" and "Factors Related to Human Health" in Table 3.3, as follows:

Table 3.3 CEPH Draft Revisions (2016)

Category	Foundational Public Health Knowledge
Profession and Science of Public Health	1. Explain public health history, philosophy, and values
	2. Identify the core functions of public health and the Ten Essential Services
	3. Use the science of epidemiology to describe and assess a population's health
	4. List major causes and trends of morbidity and mortality in the U.S. or other community relevant to the school/program
	5. Discuss the science of prevention at all levels, including health promotion, screening, etc.
	6. Explain the use of informatics in public health
	7. Identify strategies for promoting health equity
Factors Related to Human Health	8. Explain effects of environmental factors on human health
	9. Explain biological and genetic factors that impact human health
	10. Explain behavioral and psychological factors that impact human behavior
	11. Explain the social, political, and economic determinants of health and health inequities
	12. Explain the impact of globalization and the global burden of disease
	13. Explain a One-Health, ecological perspective on the connections among human health, animal health, and ecosystem health

The proposed revisions to the "foundational" (previously "core") public health knowledge areas highlight important modifications to existing curricula. Specifically, the incorporation of informatics as a new discipline begs the question of how data collection, analysis, and interpretation—traditionally left to foundational coursework in biostatistics—may now either be supplanted by formal coursework in informatics, or complemented by the same insofar as informatics is integrated within existing biostatistics courses. (The latter is unlikely given the sheer breadth and depth of informatics-related content that would make a single module on the same useless for all practical purposes.) A challenge of securing foundational knowledge is the range of expectations, including familiarity with specific frameworks (e.g. "Ten Essential Public Health Services") and disciplines (e.g. use the science of epidemiology), to general knowledge (e.g. explain social determinants and the impact of globalization).

Any attempt to create a model public health curriculum will be in vain, but there are opportunities to utilize these developments to refine existing curricula. For example, consider the generic "core" curriculum pattern in Table 3.4.

Table 3.4 Sample MPH Core Curriculum

Sample MPH Core Curriculum: Epidemiology Concentration	Credits
Introduction to Public Health	4
Biostatistics	4
Epidemiology I	4
Epidemiology II	4
Social and Behavioral Health	4
Environmental Health Sciences	4
Health Services Administration	4
Scientific Writing	2
Foundational Total	30

A proposed revision of the core curriculum is provided below, with corresponding notes and explanations thereafter.

Proposed Foundational Coursework: All Concentrations	Credits
Introduction to Public Health	0
Biostatistics: Data Collection, Analysis, and Interpretation[1]	4
Epidemiology: Clinical, Population, and Social Dimensions[2]	4
Social and Behavioral Health	4
Environmental Health	4
Public Health Policy: Issues, Theories, and Advocacy[3]	4
Scientific Writing	2
Program Planning and Evaluation[4]	4
Leadership, Management, and Administration[5]	2
Foundational Total	28

Notes

1 The revised CEPH criteria is practice-oriented, so the emphasis should be on data collection, analysis, and interpretation, which is consistent with the skills that candidates will obtain from this course. The scope should include exploratory data analysis as well as inferential statistics, including hypothesis testing and regression (linear, multiple linear, and logistic) with familiarity with a computer software program (e.g., STATA, SAS).

2 This is perhaps the most important and most challenging foundational course owing to the unique perspectives and approaches of researchers in clinical, population, and social epidemiology. Given the heightened attention to social determinants in our public and population health discourse, and the unique considerations for clinicians and traditional public health researchers, a course that provides a common foundation of concepts and methods, and draws examples from these different domains, would be nothing short of extraordinary. I have yet to see a single introductory epidemiology course accomplish this, in large part owing to the limitations of existing textbooks that may focus on only one of these dimensions (e.g., Gordis, Kaufman, Szklo and Nieto), and therefore selecting articles and/or book chapters that can round out the educational experience would be immensely helpful, particularly for those candidates who do not specialize in epidemiology.

3 Public Health Policy is perhaps the most elusive field in public health due to the myriad of disciplines and stakeholders that influence the development and administration of policy.

Historically, health policy education in public health curricula has had a myopic focus on health economics and a splash of public policy. The content ought to be enhanced to specifically incorporate the role of Politics, Epidemiology and Medicine, Ethics, Economics, and Law (a "PEEEL" framework) with skills that enhance oral and written advocacy. The scope of the class should introduce students to an interdisciplinary framework to approach public health policy issues, and empower them with practical analytical tools to develop research policy briefs, letters to an editor, and an advocacy pitch to an elected representative.

4 This course would actually satisfy a foundational skill that CEPH has identified for all public health students in its third draft of the revised accreditation standards (D2.7-11, CEPH Revised Accreditation Criteria, 2/1/16). I therefore recommend that it be incorporated within the core requirements for all students.

5 Training in leadership is among the new foundational competencies in the latest draft of the revised accreditation standards. I propose a two-credit course with specific competencies focused on the development of national health policies (based on the APHA process for interdisciplinary teams at the national level), and strategic plans, which is explicitly noted in the revised criteria (D3.5, CEPH Revised Accreditation Criteria, 2/1/16).

As we see above, a curriculum can be enhanced in its scope and content and even end up costing fewer credits, resulting in cost-savings for the student. With skyrocketing costs in graduate education, it is essential to ensure that the curricula are lean and afford an exceptional return on investment by aligning them with the precise domains, standards, and criteria of the accrediting bodies.

The alignment of standards and domains is an iterative process. The PHAB domains, for example, built upon the 10 Essential Public Health Services, were developed by the Core Public Health Functions Steering Committee in 1994, as indicated in Table 3.5.

Table 3.5 PHAB Domains and 10 Essential Public Health Services

PHAB	10 Essential Public Health Services (1994)
1. Conduct and disseminate assessments focused on population health status and public health issues facing the community	1. Monitor health status to identify and solve community health problems
2. Investigate health problems and environmental public health hazards to protect the community	2. Diagnose and investigate health problems and health hazards in the community
3. Inform and educate about public health issues and functions	3. Inform, educate, and empower people about health issues
4. Engage with the community to identify and address health problems	4. Mobilize community partnerships and action to identify and solve health problems
5. Develop public health policies and plans	5. Develop policies and plans that support individual and community health efforts
6. Enforce public health laws	6. Enforce laws and regulations that protect health and ensure safety

PHAB	10 Essential Public Health Services (1994)
7. Promote strategies to improve access to healthcare	7. Link people to needed personal health services and assure the provision of healthcare when otherwise unavailable
8. Maintain a competent public health workforce	8. Assure competent public and personal healthcare workforce
9. Evaluate and continuously improve processes, programs, and interventions	9. Evaluate effectiveness, accessibility, and quality of personal and population-based health services
10. Contribute to and apply the evidence base of public health	10. Research for new insights and innovative solutions to health problems
11. *Maintain administrative and management capacity*	
12. *Maintain capacity to engage the public health governing entity*	

Although domains 1 through 10 are essentially mirror images of the 10 Essential Public Health Services, the inclusion of domains 11 and 12 within the PHAB are particularly noteworthy. Domain 11 addresses administrative and management capacity, including the development and maintenance of an operational infrastructure, and the establishment of effective financial management systems. Domain 12 addresses governance, specifically maintaining current operational definitions and standards (including statements of roles, responsibilities, and authorities); providing information to the governing entity regarding public health and official responsibilities of the health department; and encouraging that entity's engagement in the department's overall obligations and responsibilities.

Beyond revising the core knowledge, the revised CEPH criteria have created "Foundational Competencies" which are informed by the prior core knowledge areas and cross-cutting and emerging public health areas. Among these competencies are Program Planning and Management, as well as Leadership, which can be aligned with the PHAB domains as indicated in Table 3.6 below.

Satisfying the specific standards of governance, however, is notably addressed beyond the revised Master's level criteria proposed by CEPH within its doctoral (i.e. DrPH) foundational competencies. For doctoral students, acquiring and aligning human, fiscal, and other resources to achieve strategic goals, and cultivating new resources and revenue streams to achieve those goals, are among explicit competencies within the category of "Leadership, Management and Governance."

Competencies unique to leadership may have been traditionally reserved for doctoral training, with specific deliverables including strategic

Table 3.6 PHAB and CEPH Revised Draft Accreditation Criteria, "Foundational Competencies" (2016)

PHAB	CEPH Revised Draft Criteria (2016) "Foundational Competencies"
11. Maintain administrative and management capacity	[Program Planning and Management] 9. Explain basic principles of resource management including human, fiscal, and material
12. Maintain capacity to engage the public health governing entity	[Leadership] 14. Apply principles of effective management and leadership, including fostering collaboration, guiding decision making, creating a vision, and motivating others

planning, operational planning, and fiscal management. Deliberation among faculty members as to the appropriate content in introductory and advanced level coursework is a perpetual discussion at the graduate level. The advent of baccalaureate programs in public health or related programs in health studies, along with the advent of public health credentialing and specifically the recent development of revised eligibility criteria, presents novel issues for consideration.

Professional training in allied fields of medicine, nursing, and law must ultimately prepare candidates for professional licensure, thereby standardizing education and training along the precise domains and standards of competencies that will be subsequently tested by a state governing body. In public health, however, no such licensure exists.

The development of the Certified in Public Health (CPH) credential by the National Board of Public Health Examiners was intended to address this gap by explicitly creating a "national, professional standard" that would "increase recognition of the public health professions" and "advance cohesiveness and collaboration with ... professional peers."[1]

The credential is afforded to candidates who have successfully completed or concurrently enrolled in a CEPH-accredited graduate degree, or who have taken the "core" courses (epidemiology, biostatistics, behavioral sciences/health education, environmental health, health administration/policy) and have a relevant graduate degree, along with three years of public health work experience.[2]

The scope of the examination includes assessment of the five core knowledge areas from the old CEPH criteria (2011) along with "cross-cutting" areas, summarized in Table 3.7 below.

While the scope of the exam may have been adequate based on the original CEPH criteria (2011), the proposed revisions profoundly change the appropriate scope of credentialing given the expansion of foundational areas of knowledge and competencies. While the five traditional disciplines

Table 3.7 NBPHE CPH Exam

Content Area	Percentage of the CPH Exam	Approximate # Questions Based on 200-Question Exam
General Principles	12.5%	25
Health Policy and Management	15%	30
Environmental Health Sciences	15%	30
Epidemiology	15%	30
Social Behavioral Sciences	15%	30
Cross-cutting	12.5%	25
Communication and Informatics	[1.7%]	[3.5]
Diversity and Culture	[1.7%]	[3.5]
Leadership	[1.7%]	[3.5]
Ethics and Professionalism	[1.7%]	[3.5]
Program Planning and Evaluation	[1.7%]	[3.5]
Public Health Biology	[1.7%]	[3.5]
Systems Thinking	[1.7%]	[3.5]

facilitated the allocation of questions to those areas, their absence, or more accurately their integration within a broader array of learning objectives and competencies, requires a significant overhaul of this framework to address numerous factors related to the profession and science of public health, factors related to human health, and the extensive list of foundational competencies. Examples include the explanation of public health philosophy and values; the impact of globalization and the global burden of disease; political and economic determinants; principles of resource management; and interprofessional practice, specifically performing effectively on interprofessional teams. Even in its current form, the allocation of a handful of questions to effectively address competencies in critical areas of leadership, culture and diversity, and ethics and professionalism, is woefully inadequate.

In addition to the number of topical areas and the appropriate allocation of questions is a recognition that this assessment is detached from practice. While medical students and residents are evaluated in their actual interaction with patients, we do not have an equivalent assessment of communication and interprofessional practice. If we expect candidates to develop technical or professional papers on public health issues or deliver oral presentations on the same—per the revised draft CEPH Foundational Competencies 17 and 18—credentialing may need to move beyond a multiple-choice and theory-driven model of test-taking.

Another development that raises numerous issues is the revision of the eligibility criteria. Previously, only individuals who had obtained a graduate degree from a CEPH-accredited program were eligible for the exam. However, the credential was recently extended to individuals who only have a Bachelor's degree and five years of public health work experience, "indicating the scope of foundational knowledge that has been acquired based on the ten essential public health services." Notably, there is no explicit requirement that the Bachelor's degree should be in public health. Among the questions that ought to be addressed include whether individuals with a Bachelor's degree in public health will be eligible for the exam, irrespective of their subsequent years of public health work experience.

III. Conclusion

Against this backdrop and cursory review of the standards and domains of accreditation for health departments, the current and proposed accreditation criteria for public health educational programs, and the credentialing of public health professionals, we have identified numerous issues and opportunities to refine and enhance our assessment tools to evaluate the requisite skills and competencies of our current (and future) public health professionals. It is imperative for leaders within health departments, schools, and training programs to critically examine these different instruments to ensure that our future generation of public health professionals are adequately prepared to execute their roles and responsibilities to advance population health.

Appendix 1. Public Health Accreditation Board (PHAB) Domains and Standards for Health Departments[3]

Domain 1 "Assess"	Conduct and disseminate assessments focused on population health status and public health issues facing the community.
Standard	1.1 Participate in or Lead a Collaborative Process Resulting in a Comprehensive Community Health Assessment
	1.2 Collect and Maintain Reliable, Comparable, and Valid Data that Provide Information on Conditions of Public Health Importance and on the Health Status of the Population.
	1.3 Analyze Public Health Data to Identify Trends in Health Problems, Environmental Public Health Hazards, and Social and Economic Factors that Affect the Public's Health
	1.4 Provide and Use the Results of Health Data Analysis to Develop Recommendations Regarding Public Health Policy, Processes, Programs, or Interventions

Domain 2 "Investigate"	Investigate health problems and environmental public health hazards to protect the community
	2.1 Conduct Timely Investigations of Health Problems and Environmental Public Health Hazards
	2.2 Contain/Mitigate Health Problems and Environmental Public Health Hazards
	2.3 Ensure Access to Laboratory and Epidemiologic/Environmental Public Health Expertise and Capacity to Investigate and Contain/Mitigate Public Health Problems and Environmental Public Health Hazards
	2.4 Maintain a Plan with Policies and Procedures for Urgent and Non-Urgent Communications
Domain 3 "Inform and Educate"	Inform and educate about public health issues and functions
	3.1 Provide Health Education and Health Promotion Policies, Programs, Processes, and Interventions to Support Prevention and Wellness
	3.2 Provide Information on Public Health Issues and Public Health Functions Through Multiple Methods to a Variety of Audiences
Domain 4 "Community Engagement"	Engage with the community to identify and address health problems
	4.1 Engage with the Public Health System and the Community in Identifying and Addressing Health Problems through Collaborative Processes
	4.2 Promote the Community's Understanding of and Support for Policies and Strategies that will Improve the Public's Health
Domain 5 "Policies and Plans"	Develop public health policies and plans
	5.1 Serve as a Primary and Expert Resource for Establishing and Maintaining Public Health Policies, Practices, and Capacity
	5.2 Conduct a Comprehensive Planning Process Resulting in a Tribal/State/Community Health Improvement Plan
	5.3 Develop and Implement a Health Department Organizational Strategic Plan
	5.4 Maintain an All Hazards Emergency Operations Plan

Domain 6 "Public Health Laws"	Enforce public health laws	
	6.1	Review Existing Laws and Work with Governing Entities and Elected/Appointed Officials to Update as Needed
	6.2	Educate Individuals and Organizations on the Meaning, Purpose, and Benefit of Public Health Laws and How to Comply
	6.3	Conduct and Monitor Public Health Enforcement Activities and Coordinate Notification of Violations among Appropriate Agencies
Domain 7 "Access to Care"	Promote strategies to improve access to health care	
	7.1	Assess Health Care Service Capacity and Access to Health Care Services
	7.2	Identify and Implement Strategies to Improve Access to Health Care Services
Domain 8 "Workforce"	Maintain a competent public health workforce	
	8.1	Encourage the Development of a Sufficient Number of Qualified Public Health Workers
	8.2	Ensure a Competent Workforce through Assessment of Staff Competencies, the Provision of Individual Training and Professional Development, and the Provision of a Supportive Work Environment
Domain 9 "Quality Improvement"	Evaluate and continuously improve processes, programs, and interventions	
	9.1	Use a Performance Management System to Monitor Achievement of Organizational Objectives
	9.2	Develop and Implement Quality Improvement Processes Integrated into Organizational Practice, Programs, Processes, and Interventions
Domain 10 "Evidence-Based Practices"	Contribute to and apply the evidence base of public health	
	10.1	Identify and Use the Best Available Evidence for Making Informed Public Health Practice Decisions
	10.2	Promote Understanding and Use of the Current Body of Research Results, Evaluations, and Evidence-Based Practices with Appropriate Audiences

Domain 11 "Administration and Management"	Maintain administrative and management capacity	
	11.1	Develop and Maintain an Operational Infrastructure to Support the Performance of Public Health Functions
	11.2	Establish Effective Financial Management Systems
Domain 12 "Governance"	Maintain capacity to engage the public health governing entity	
	12.1	Maintain Current Operational Definitions and Statements of the Public Health Roles, Responsibilities, and Authorities
	12.2	Provide Information to the Governing Entity Regarding Public Health and the Official Responsibilities of the Health Department and of the Governing Entity
	12.3	Encourage the Governing Entity's Engagement in the Public Health Department's Overall Obligations and Responsibilities

Notes

1   https://www.nbphe.org/getcertified.cfm
2   https://www.nbphe.org/eligibility.cfm
3   http://www.phaboard.org/wp-content/uploads/SM-Version-1.5-Board-adopted-FINAL-01-24-2014.docx.pdf

Part II

Post-Affordable Care Act Challenges and Opportunities

4 Novel Interprofessional Collaborations

Utilizing Medical–Legal Partnerships to Advance Population Health

Dru Bhattacharya, JD, MPH, LLM and Jay Bhatt, DO, MPH, MPA, FACP

I. Introduction

One of the most important national initiatives to target settings that care for large proportions of disadvantaged populations is the Health Disparities Collaboratives sponsored by the Health Resources and Services Administration (HRSA). These collaboratives comprise community health centers that are brought together to learn and disseminate quality-improvement techniques developed by the Institute for Healthcare Improvement. At least one controlled pre-intervention and post-intervention study of community health centers, participating in quality-improvement collaboratives, demonstrated considerably greater improvement than the external and internal control centers in the composite measures of quality for the care of patients with asthma (Bashir 2002).

II. Medical-Legal Partnership

An emerging, albeit distinct, collaborative is the medical-legal partnership (MLP), which comprises community health centers partnered with a legal clinic that specializes in social determinants of health. In the United States there are at least 119 hospitals, 112 health centers, 30 health schools, 88 legal agencies, 37 law schools, and 66 pro bono partners that have developed MLPs to help children, the elderly, veterans, and individuals afflicted with chronic illnesses (Sinai Urban Health Institute 2004).

Patients are referred by their physician to the legal clinic's staff and attorneys to discuss legal issues identified by the provider that may be related to the patient's underlying health condition. Exposure to environmental hazards that are in violation of housing codes, subjecting residents to harmful toxins, is an example of an issue that may cause or exacerbate particular ailments such as asthma.

To date, however, there has been no exploration of utilizing the MLP as a locus of research and intervention. Some MLPs are developed in collaboration with universities, and particularly legal clinics within a school of law. For example, the Health Justice Project (HJP) is an interdisciplinary MLP between Loyola University Chicago School of Law and Erie Family Health Center, comprising fifteen community-based health centers in Chicagoland, to provide free legal assistance to Erie patients to overcome the social, legal, and systemic barriers that prevent long-term health and stability for low-income individuals and families in Chicago. Erie serves 40,000 patients annually through 148,000 visits. The patients are 68% women, 79% Hispanic, 31% uninsured, and 83% live below the Federal Poverty Line. Case management services are available for children with asthma, notwithstanding the existing trends. The HJP focuses exclusively on providing legal assistance to clients that have suffered from identifiable social determinants of health for which the law provides some remedy.

This chapter draws from my experience as an advisor and researcher for the Health Justice Project, and information obtained through interviews with the former Managing Deputy Commissioner and Chief Strategy and Innovation Officer of the Chicago Department of Public Health to identify precisely how to establish meaningful collaboration among legal and healthcare practitioners to advance population health. Upon reflection, I propose a sample research project with requisite specificity that illustrates how we may effectively utilize medical-legal partnerships to advance population health. Specifically, my proposed project focuses on implementing an in-client educational program to incentivize patient adherence to management guidelines for asthma.

To date, the precise association of the underlying environmental and socio-economic determinants with health ailments has not taken account of patient adherence to care management guidelines. For asthmatic patients, adherence rates have been estimated to be below 50%, and the implementation of individualized educational programs (IEPs) has been successful for hospitalized cohorts of patients who presented in response to emergent attacks. Most providers in community health centers, however, are overworked and underpaid, creating little time or incentive to implement an IEP for every patient. The role of MLPs as a locus of research and intervention has not been explored and affords an opportunity to improve patient adherence and care. The MLP staff would be capable of providing the time to simultaneously reinforce guidelines for adherence and afford an indirect monetary incentive by way of legal representation for mitigating existing social determinants of health for which the law may provide a remedy. While representation would not be contingent upon the patient adhering to the guidelines, it is plausible that patients would be more likely to entertain such advice from an individual who may secure tangible monetary rewards for the patient that may, or may not, be related to the underlying health condition. Notably, an interesting peripheral research inquiry is whether patient adherence is on the causal pathway of the association between the precise social determinants for which the law provides a remedy for poor housing and recurrent health events.

By retrospectively estimating the association of social correlates and health events, along with a prospective cohort study of an ICEP to improve patient adherence, we can potentially demonstrate the utility of aligning the MLP with a key priority (respiratory health) identified by the CHNAs and consequently serve as a locus of research and intervention to improve health outcomes. In the absence of explicit guidance on how to translate findings from CHNAs into interventions or partnerships that may improve health outcomes, physicians and hospitals are left with no recourse to act upon such assessments. This kind of study may fill this gap by illustrating the utility of the MLP to identify and respond to the precise needs of the most vulnerable populations within a community and encourage hospitals to create or collaborate with legal clinics to secure population health.

A. General Goals

From 2001 to 2011 the number of persons with asthma in the U.S. increased by 28%, yet the adherence rate is currently estimated at under 50% for adults and 40% among children (Centers for Disease Control and Prevention 2013). The attendant costs include medical expenses ($50.1 billion per year), loss of productivity from missed school or work days ($3.8 billion per year), and premature death ($2.1 billion per year), totalling over $56 billion annually (Centers for Disease Control and Prevention 2013). Still, these national trends are not homogenous. Death rates from asthma are four to six times higher for African-Americans and Hispanics compared to non-Hispanic Whites, and are concentrated in urban areas (U.S. Department of Health and Human Services 2012). Puerto Rican children have the highest asthma prevalence rate (34%) in Chicago compared to a national average of 10% among children of all races (U.S. Department of Health and Human Services 2012). Additionally, substandard housing has been shown to be associated with asthma but this is also not evenly distributed, disproportionately affecting low-income and African-American populations who are 1.7 times and 2.2 times more likely to occupy homes with severe physical problems respectively, compared to the general population (Krieger and Higgins 2002).

In an effort to align hospital services with these unmet population health needs, the Patient Protection and Affordable Care Act (ACA) mandates that all 501(c)(3) non-profit hospital organizations should conduct a community health needs assessment (CHNA) in each taxable year and adopt an implementation strategy to meet those needs identified through the assessment. Such organizations must take into account input from persons who represent the broad interests of the community served by the hospital facility, including those with special knowledge of, or expertise in, public health, and also ensure that the assessment be made widely available to the public. Aligning the CHNAs with targeted interventions, however, remains a pressing concern.

Mechanistic hypotheses explaining disparities in health outcomes or determinants as being attributable, in part, to disproportionate exposure to social or environmental triggers are incomplete owing to their failure to account for the adequacy of care management and patient adherence. For example, individual susceptibility to asthma attacks is partly due to lasting effects of inadequate adherence to management guidelines, including appropriate metered-dose inhaler administration technique, awareness of early warning signs, and timely execution of action plans. Additional factors include social determinants, such as health literacy, medical transportation, and access to care (Bauman, Wright, Leickly et al. 2002). Thus, urban low-income populations residing in substandard housing may be unable to adapt because of the resultant—or independent— role of failing to adhere to management guidelines for asthma (Bashir 2002; Martin, Catrambone, Kee et al. 2013; Paasche-Orlow, Riekert, Bilderback et al. 2005).

Over time, the community health center has emerged as an effective stakeholder to alleviate the burden of illness among low-income and ethnic minority populations (George, O'Dowd, Martin, et al. 1999; Martin, Catrambone, Kee et al. 2013). One strategy to reduce the burden of illness in these populations is a comprehensive educational program that improves clinical outcome measures. The development of an inpatient educational program (IEP) for hospitalized patients has been shown to yield higher follow-up rates compared with outpatient appointments, and significantly fewer emergency department visits and hospitalizations for asthma in the six months following IEP intervention, as compared to the control population (Martin, Catrambone, Kee et al. 2013). Similar programs have been successfully implemented for managing diabetes (Hicks, O'Malley, Lieu et al. 2010), congestive heart failure (Munoz, Pronovost, Dintzis et al. 2012), and obesity.

We may test the relevance of the IEP to the potential role of medical-legal partnerships (MLP) as a locus of research and intervention to align patient-client services in response to a key priority—respiratory health— identified by CHNAs to alleviate the burden of illness among non-hospitalized, low-income referrals. Respiratory health ailments, including asthma, have been identified as a key priority by health departments such as the Chicago Department of Public Health (CDPH), after conducting a thorough review of the CHNAs made available by sixteen Chicago hospitals in response to the federal mandate.

My hypothesis is that the development of an in-client (as opposed to inpatient) educational program (ICEP) for non-hospitalized patients with asthma referred to the MLP will: (1) experience fewer adverse health events; and (2) require fewer visits to a provider on account of such adverse events (i.e. not routine follow-up), as compared to the control population.

B. Specific Goals

1 Retrospectively determine whether there is an association between social correlates for which the law provides a remedy (e.g. poor housing conditions), and the presence or absence of the morbidity (i.e. asthma) among patients referred to the MLP over the prior three years, and any disparities on account of race or other demographic factors.

 Hypothesis: There is an association between social correlates and the presence or absence of asthma among patients referred to an MLP that disproportionately affect African-Americans and Hispanics who also experience higher rates of social obstacles to health compared to non-Hispanic Whites.

2 Prospectively assess whether African-American and Hispanic asthmatic patients referred to an MLP and afforded an ICEP experience improved adherence rates, fewer adverse health events, and fewer visits to a provider on account of such adverse events (i.e. not routine follow-up) as compared to the control population.

 Hypothesis: Patients with an ICEP experience higher adherence rates, fewer adverse events, and fewer visits to a provider on account of such adverse events compared to patients who do not receive an ICEP.

C. Plan of Action

To accomplish these aims, we will:

1 Conduct a retrospective case-series study of, say, 1000 adult and adolescent patients who were clients of an MLP over a specified time period (e.g. 2000–2015) to estimate the risk of patients exposed to environmental and social correlates. Each of these encounters have been documented with the requisite information on social correlates and the patient's morbidity, and is on file with the investigators.

2 Conduct a prospective eighteen-month cohort study of 180 participants with 90 subjects randomized to either an in-client educational program (ICEP) along with a screening of social obstacles to care, *or* only screened for social obstacles with no attendant ICEP. We shall subsequently assess adherence rates based on direct and indirect measures, which will be utilized to assess the effectiveness of the ICEP to increase adherence rates, and reduce adverse events and healthcare utilization. We suggest follow-up at six, twelve, and eighteen months, consistent with primary care management guidelines that recommend follow-up once every six months for patients taking low doses of inhaled corticosteroid.

D. Composition of the Interprofessional Research Team

The project investigators and collaborators ought to be experienced scholars and practitioners in medicine, public health, law, and epidemiology, making them well positioned to address the present need for, and implementation of, the current project. In practice, this would entail at least three leadership roles: the clinician overseeing the delivery of care for the patient, the attorney overseeing advocacy on behalf of the patient-client, and a researcher overseeing the collection, analysis, interpretation, and dissemination of data.

E. Preliminary Data

Pilot data collected independently by health departments and MLPs may provide insight into the unmet needs and the precise scope of services that ought to be rendered to the affected population. For example, the Chicago Department of Public Health (CDPH) and Loyola University Chicago's Health Justice Project have spearheaded initiatives over the years to accumulate preliminary data on CHNAs and the unmet needs of clients served by MLPs through Illinois, respectively. The findings are summarized below, and demonstrate the pressing need and opportunity to align the legal mandate of CHNAs with the services of MLPs to promote population health.

III. Chicago Department of Public Health Assessment of Sixteen Chicago CHNAs

In March 2014 the CDPH released a report summarizing its review of CHNAs conducted by sixteen Chicago hospitals as of September 2013, identifying the key findings and priority health issues emerging from the assessment. For each priority, CDPH cited the best practices and interventions based on the U.S. Centers for Disease Prevention and Control's *Guide to Community Preventive Services*, which is informed by the CDC-appointed Community Preventive Services Task Force. Notably, case management is among the recommendations for many ailments, including respiratory health.

A. Health Justice Project Survey of Patients' Needs and Services of MLPs in Illinois

In April 2014, Bhattacharya et al. completed a survey of clients' needs and services offered by MLPs throughout Illinois. The survey was conducted from February 2014 through June 2014, and sampled representatives from ten MLPs in Illinois. Representatives were selected based on their current participation on the MLP Advisory Committee or based on prior involvement with its efforts. Survey responses were obtained from ten representatives (100%) of: SSI Homeless Outreach Project, Health Disparities Project, Metro East Medical Legal Partnership, NIU College of Law Health Advocacy Clinic, AIDS Legal Council of Chicago, Chicago Medical–Legal Partnership for Children, Medical Legal Partnership of Southern Illinois, MLP-Peoria Area, East Central Illinois MLP, and Loyola University Chicago School of Law Health Justice Project. Surveys were conducted using SurveyMonkey® and data were managed and analyzed with STATA version 12.1 (StataCorp LP, College Station, TX). Maps of counties, poverty rates, and major health needs were generated using Microsoft MapPoint®.

Demographic characteristics were summarized in a table, reprinted below:

Table 4.1 Demographic Characteristics of Respondents and Communities for the Survey

	Service Area				Racial Constituency (%) of the Counties Served		
Name	Counties Served	Population	Avg. Med. Income ($)	Avg. Med Poverty (%)	White	Black	Hispanic
SSI Homeless	2	5,255,610	51,522	16	44	25	25
Health Disparities	1	5,240,700	54,648	16	43	25	25
Metro East	6	407,753	54,783	15	73	21	3
NIU	3	1,575,117	77,016	8	66	5	20
AIDS Legal	1	5,240,700	54,648	16	43	25	25
Chicago MLP	1	5,240,700	54,648	16	43	25	25
Southern Illinois	8	275,916	40,376	19	87	7	3
Peoria	6	387,915	55,580	13	84	9	3
East Central	14	528,856	44,333	11	83	4	2
Loyola	1	5,240,700	54,648	16	43	25	25
MLP totals*	39	8,431,167					
State totals**	102	12,882,135	56,853	13.7	63	14.8	16.3

Notes
* The total counties and population includes only distinct counties and residents so that a county served by more than one MLP was not counted more than once for the purpose of estimating the total count.
** State totals based on the most recent estimates reported by the U.S. Census Bureau.

Table 4.2 Characteristics of Communities Served by Respondent MLPs

Name	Service Area			Racial Constituency (%) of the Clients Serviced		
	Years in Service	Clients (Total)	Clients (Avg. Annual)	White	Black	Hispanic
SSI Homeless	8.5	4,300	750	13	56	28
Health Disparities	1	5,240	4,648	43	25	25
NIU	1	111	100	59	36	2
AIDS Legal	23	>2,500*	320	16	54	27
Southern Illinois	12	1,921	200	87	7	3
Peoria	8	1,148	200	70	30	–
Loyola	4	1,536	410	5	9	81
Total of Ranges	(1, 23)	16,756	(100, 4648)	(5, 87)	(7, 56)	(0, 81)

Note
* Legal outreach work at Fantus Clinic (and later the CORE Centre) first opened its doors in 1991, though unduplicated counts going back to 1991 are unavailable.

Notable findings include the diversity of medical departments that refer patients to MLPs, and the pressing health needs that are consistent with the key priorities identified by CHD above.

Respondents represented ten MLPs that served thirty-nine counties across the state of Illinois, including the northern, central, eastern, and southern regions of the state (Figure 4.1). Socioeconomic disparities were not unique to any specific region, but there was a consistent presence of MLPs within those counties with more concentrated rates of poverty. Counties were stratified in three categories based on the percentage of households below the federal poverty rate for 2008–2012 (<10%, 10–19%, and 20–30%); we observed higher rates of poverty (20–30%) in the southern and eastern regions of the state, while households with incomes below 20% of the poverty level were dispersed throughout the southern, central, and northern counties (Figure 4.2).

Notably, over 85% of the participants identified federally qualified health centers among the sources of patient referrals to their MLP. Additionally, over sixteen distinct medical specialties were identified, suggesting that the MLP is not limited in serving a distinct health condition but may be utilized by all hospitals to serve the unmet needs of vulnerable populations. Social structure operates along distinct pathways, including material, occupational, and social/environmental factors that affect health outcomes and well-being. Among the pressing health needs identified by the MLPs participating in the survey are respiratory infections, including asthma and chronic obstructive pulmonary disease.

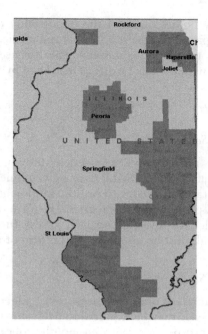

Figure 4.1 Counties Served by 10 MLPs

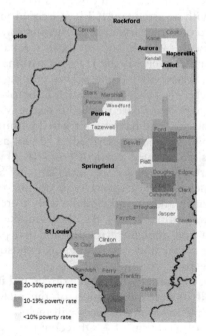

Figure 4.2 Poverty Rates of Counties

These preliminary findings suggest the opportunity of identifying the MLP as a powerful partner to assist hospitals and medical departments to respond effectively to unmet community health needs identified by CHNAs, consistent with the key priorities identified by CDPH, above.

B. Research Methods

Retrospective Case-Series Study

Participants in the retrospective case-series study might include the patients who were referred to an MLP over a given time period, and who self-reported their status as relates to health, employment, housing, and other socio-demographic indicators on an intake form that is on file with the MLP and to which the investigators have access. Institutional Review Board (IRB) approval must be obtained for this arm of the study.

Prospective Cohort Study

There are no gold standard objective measures of adherence, and patient self-reports of adherence may be expected to overestimate adherence. We might conduct a prospective eighteen-month cohort study of 180 participants randomized equally (i.e. ninety subjects in each arm) to either ICEP, along with a screening of social obstacles to care *or* only screened for social obstacles with no attendant ICEP. We could subsequently assess adherence rates based on direct and indirect measures appropriate to each health condition. The MLP staff and the health department will work closely to develop and implement the IEPs for asthma. With respect to asthma, inclusion criteria will include adolescents aged 10 to 17 and adults 18 and over who meet the standard definition of asthma, and have been referred by their primary care physician to the MLP. Additionally, they should live in the city, and have been treated within the past year for an asthma exacerbation and prescribed a daily asthma controller medication, such as an inhaled corticosteroid (ICS) or a leukotriene modifier (LM). Participants may be English- or Spanish-speaking. Exclusion criteria included adolescents who do not meet the age and residency requirements, and/or individuals who were participating in another asthma intervention study. At client intake, MLP staff will interview the patient and implement the IEP for that particular ailment, and obtain data on social and environmental exposures (e.g. housing conditions and allergens).

At each follow-up, outcomes will include direct and indirect measures. Direct measures will include observation of the metered-dose inhaler (MDI) technique, while indirect measures will include self-reporting and asthma diaries. The observation of MDI technique will require trained staff to document appropriate inhaler use based on the Inhaler Use

Checklist. Self-reporting may be conducted by MLP staff by interview or paper-and-pencil measures that request patients to recall levels and patterns of medication over each six-month period (e.g. Medical Adherence Scale or Inhaler Adherence Scale), while asthma diaries may include daily diaries in which patients record medication use and symptoms (Rand and Wise 1994).

Caregivers or adults might be compensated $10 at the initial intake and at each subsequent follow-up at six-month, twelve-month, and eighteen-month intervals, totaling $40 if (s)he completes all four intervention visits. The study would be submitted for review by each site's institutional review board with informed consent obtained from all adults and caregivers.

The estimated population mean adherence rate within the general population is approximately 50% with a standard deviation of 25% (Munoz, Pronovost, Dintzis et al. 2012). We estimate that ethnic minorities will have a mean adherence rate of 38.5%. We conducted a power calculation for a comparison of proportions and found that a sample size of 144 achieves at least 80% power to detect that the proportion is different from urban ethnic minorities, given a significance level (alpha) of 0.05. Since we anticipate a maximum of 20% dropout rate, we intend to enroll 180 participants evenly distributed across the ICEP and control groups.

C. Statistical Analyses

For the retrospective study, data will be collated and grouped in the categories listed above, initially drawn from individual intake forms and then pooled to look for any ecological differences based on the strength of association between the different social correlates and diagnosed morbidities among patients referred to the MLP. The statistical analyses will include a combination of descriptive measures and, where appropriate, analysis of proportions and the impact of multiple predictors, including employment, housing conditions, financial and educational status, and other social variables, all of which are recorded on the intake form and available to the investigators. Data will be presented as means ± standard errors. Differences will be significant at an alpha p-level of <0.05. Comparisons of proportions will be conducted using Chi-Square analysis (X^2) to examine, for example, whether referrals with particular social correlates experience particular morbidities than referrals without such correlates.

For the prospective study we shall employ descriptive statistics, as well as X^2 in bivariate analysis to assess whether referrals with an ICEP experience fewer adverse health events and fewer visits to a provider on account of such adverse events as compared to the control population. Logistic regression models will also be used to control for confounding

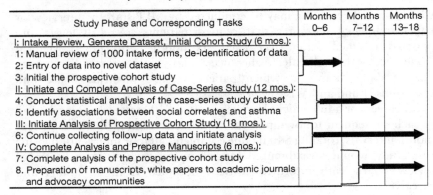

Study Phase and Corresponding Tasks	Months 0–6	Months 7–12	Months 13–18
I: Intake Review, Generate Dataset, Initial Cohort Study (6 mos.):			
1: Manual review of 1000 intake forms, de-identification of data			
2: Entry of data into novel dataset			
3: Initial the prospective cohort study			
II: Initiate and Complete Analysis of Case-Series Study (12 mos.):			
4: Conduct statistical analysis of the case-series study dataset			
5: Identify associations between social correlates and asthma			
III: Initiate Analysis of Prospective Cohort Study (18 mos.):			
6: Continue collecting follow-up data and initiate analysis			
IV: Complete Analysis and Prepare Manuscripts (6 mos.):			
7: Complete analysis of the prospective cohort study			
8: Preparation of manuscripts, white papers to academic journals and advocacy communities			

Figure 4.3 Study Phase and Corresponding Tasks

and investigate interactions. A two-sample t-test will also be utilized to determine the difference in mean adverse health events and visits to a provider among referrals with and without an ICEP.

D. *Timeline*

The project may be divided into four phases over a period of eighteen months, with corresponding tasks as described in Figure 4.3.

IV. Conclusion

While public health education may be interdisciplinary across foundational subjects (e.g. biostatistics, epidemiology, health services administration, social and behavioral health, and environmental health), the need for precise interprofessional team building, project development, and implementation have all been inadequately addressed through formal curricula and related training. MLPs offer a unique opportunity and a compelling reason to address health disparities and potentially influence public health policy. The latter, of course, is based on the development of research teams that may cull meaningful and actionable data from access to the vast array of information that may be gleaned from these collaborations. Here, we focused narrowly on utilizing medical-legal partnerships to implement an in-client educational program to incentivize patient adherence to management guidelines for asthma. In doing so, we illustrate how MLPs are a novel interprofessional collaboration that holds much promise in advancing population health, which ought to be further developed in partnership with hospitals and health departments.

References

Anderson, C.A., B.V. Deepak, Y. Amoateng-Adjepong et al. 2005. Benefits of comprehensive inpatient education and discharge planning combined with outpatient support in elderly patients with congestive heart failure. *Congestive Heart Failure* 11(6): 315–321.

Bashir, S.A. 2002. Home is where the harm is: Inadequate housing as a public health crisis. *Am J Public Health*. 92(5): 733–738.

Bauman, L.J., E. Wright, F.E. Leickly et al. 2002. Relationship of adherence to pediatric asthma morbidity among inner-city children. *Pediatrics*. 110: 6.

Centers for Disease Control and Prevention. 2013. *Asthma Facts: CDC's National Asthma Control Program Grantees*.

George, M.R., L.C. O'Dowd, I. Martin et al. 1999. A comprehensive educational program improves clinical outcome measures in inner-city patients with asthma. *Arch Intern Med*. 159: 1710–1716.

Hicks, L.S., J. O'Malley, T.A. Lieu et al. 2010. Impact of Health Disparities Collaboratives on racial/ethnic and insurance disparities in U.S. community health centers. *Arch Intern Med*. 170(3): 279–286.

Krieger, J. and D.L. Higgins. 2002. Housing and Health: Time Again for Public Health Action. *Am J Public Health*. 92: 758–768.

Martin, M.A., C.D. Catrambone, R.A. Kee et al. 2013. Home asthma triggers: Barriers to asthma control in Chicago Puerto Rican children. *Journal of Health Care for the Poor and Underserved*. 24(2): 813–827

Munoz M., P. Pronovost, J. Dintzis et al. 2012. Implementing and evaluating a multicomponent inpatient diabetes management program: Putting research into practice. *Jt Comm J Quality Patient Saf*. May; 38(5): 195–206.

Paasche-Orlow, M.K., K.A. Riekert, A. Bilderback et al. 2005. Tailored education may reduce health literacy disparities in asthma self-management. *Am J Respir Crit Care Med*. 172: 980–986.

Patient Protection and Affordable Care Act, P.L. 111-148, Section 9007(3)(A) and Section 9007(3)(B).

Rand, C.S. and R.A. Wise. 1994. Measuring adherence to asthma medication regimens. *Am J Respir Crit Care Med* 149: 569–76.

Sinai Health System, Sinai Urban Health Institute. 2004. *Improving Community Health Survey Report* 2004:1.

U.S. Department of Health and Human Services. 2012. *National Healthcare Disparities Report*. AHRQ Publication No. 12-0006. Rockville, MD.

5 From Assessment to Action

Utilizing a Game Theoretic–Epidemiological Model to Analyze Strategic Interaction and Advance Population Health

Dru Bhattacharya, JD, MPH, LLM

I. Summary

The degree of regulation and its impact on the four core focal points of public health policy—access, quality, cost, and autonomy—is exemplified by the structure, processes, and myriad of stakeholders in the legal system. Notwithstanding the passage of the Patient Protection and Affordable Care Act, however, access to care does not necessarily translate into uptake of healthcare services to secure population health. For example, the ACA requires all new private insurance plans to cover the vaccine for the human papilloma virus, which causes most cervical cancers. Yet only 54% of eligible females have obtained it. This chapter utilizes a game theoretic-epidemiological model within a medical-legal partnership to illustrate the necessity of introducing two additional focal points—corporate influence and provider conscience—alongside the traditional four focal points of healthcare policy, and provides trends in the uptake of the HPV vaccine as a case-study to demonstrate its utility.

II. Introduction

The degree of regulation and its impact on the four core focal points of public health policy—access, quality, cost, and autonomy—is exemplified by the structure, processes, and myriad of stakeholders in the legal system (Hall 2010). The seemingly rigid (but dynamic) nature of federalism, the porous separation of powers among the legislative, judicial, and executive branches of government, and the nuances of the corporate-provider-patient relationship together influence access, cost, quality, and autonomy. Notwithstanding the passage of the Patient Protection and Affordable Care Act (ACA), however, access to care does not necessarily translate into uptake of healthcare services to secure population health. For example, the ACA requires all new private insurance plans to cover the vaccine for the human papilloma virus (HPV vaccine) which causes most cervical cancers (CDC 2012). Yet between 2011 and 2012, only 54% of eligible females aged 13 to 17 received the vaccine (CDC 2013). With access, quality (i.e. the vaccine's effectiveness), and cost as supposedly non-factors in patient decision-making, the role of autonomy appears to be a dispositive issue. The promotion of private and public educational campaigns to inform parents of the benefits of the HPV vaccine is consistent with this view, but fails to capture the role and influence of third parties, namely, corporations (i.e. vaccine manufacturers) and healthcare providers.

This chapter utilizes a game theoretic-epidemiological model within a medical-legal partnership to analyze strategic interaction and advance population health. In doing so, we illustrate the necessity of introducing two additional focal points—corporate influence and provider conscience—alongside the traditional four focal points of healthcare policy, and provide trends in the uptake of the HPV vaccine as a case-study to demonstrate its utility.

III. The Unique Role of Medical-Legal Partnerships

As discussed in Chapter 5, medical-legal partnerships (MLPs) are well suited to illustrate the complexity of factors that illustrate patient decision-making owing to the inherent multidisciplinary scope of such partnerships and the particular patients/clients whom they service. MLPs are comprised of physicians and attorneys who work together to identify determinants of health for which the law provides a remedy. Therefore, physicians and attorneys must recognize the inextricable linkage of social determinants and health outcomes to identify injuries that flow from a violation of corresponding duties and rights that may implicate potential remedies for their patient-client. Furthermore, individuals who avail themselves of the services of an MLP are traditionally from low-income populations that may experience numerous barriers to care, including access, affordability, quality, and even autonomy owing to social, cultural, and linguistic barriers. This section provides an overview of a particular MLP that the author was affiliated with to provide the social context within which the proposed model and attendant methodological approaches may be employed to secure individual and population health.

The Health Justice Project (HJP) is an interdisciplinary medical-legal partnership between Loyola University Chicago School of Law and Erie Family Health Center, comprising twelve community-based health centers in Chicagoland, to provide free legal assistance to Erie patients to overcome the social, legal, and systemic barriers that prevent long-term health and stability for low-income individuals and families in Chicago. Erie serves 40,000 patients annually through 148,000 visits. The patients are 68% women, 79% Hispanic, 31% uninsured, and 83% live below the Federal Poverty Line.

The HJP focuses exclusively on providing legal assistance to clients who have suffered from identifiable social determinants of health for which the law provides some remedy. Since 2010, over 1200 patient-clients were represented, resulting in $4,230 in reduced housing expenses for clients, $561,553 in payment and forgiveness of medical expenses for clients, and $547,235 in Medicaid reimbursement to healthcare institutions based on the project's Medicaid successful denials appeals.

To date, however, the precise association of the underlying environmental and socio-economic determinants with existing health conditions has not been evaluated. Moreover, the impact of law as a preventive or remedial tool to advance individual and population health has not been measured apart from an accounting of clients who have been represented over the years. A meeting with officials from the Chicago Department of Public Health, which is authorized to craft regulations, revealed a pressing need to illustrate the effectiveness of laws and policies by providing an evidence base of outcomes that are created, sustained, and/or alleviated by modifying existing practices or behaviors.

IV. A Revised Model of Core Focal Points

Conducting empirical research in health law and management within the MLP affords an opportunity to simultaneously measure the impact of law as a preventive and remedial tool to advance individual and population health. We propose utilizing a social epidemiological paradigm, building upon a model initially crafted by physician-scientist Michael Marmot who articulated the association between social structure and health operating along three pathways, including (1) material, (2) occupational, and (3) social/environmental factors, illustrated in Figure 5.1 (Marmot and Wilkerson 2006).

In Marmot's model, factors such as access, quality, and cost are secured by the first (i.e. material) pathway with insurance coverage as their traditional proxy. Patient autonomy, however, is not merely an extension of the accessibility, acceptability, and affordability of services, respectively, but is also influenced by the social environment (the third pathway above), which encompasses corporate influence and provider conscience. Therefore, we propose the introduction of corporate influence and provider conscience as factors that bridge the material and social pathways, and which may explain trends in service uptake. Consequently, we might revise the framework consistent with the proposed model (Figure 5.2).

What Marmot's framework currently fails to capture is how information is received, interpreted, and acted upon based on existing laws and policies affecting the corporate-provider-patient relationship, and particularly the

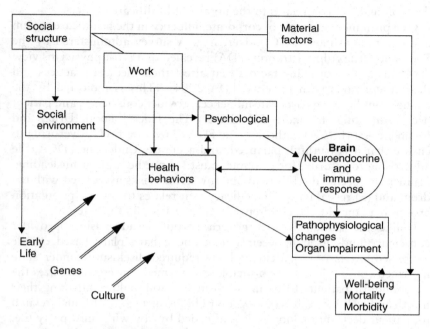

Figure 5.1 Michael Marmot's Framework of Social Determinants of Health
Source: Marmot and Wilkerson, *Social Determinants of Health*, 2006

Figure 5.2 Proposed Model of Six Focal Points of Healthcare Policy

roles of corporate influence and provider conscience, to influence patient-decision making as it relates to the uptake of healthcare services.

One prominent example of corporate influence in the healthcare system is direct-to-consumer (DTC) advertising. A survey administered by the Food and Drug Administration (FDA) revealed that most physicians view DTC ads as one of many factors that affect their medical practices and their interactions with patients (FDA 2004). (This is indicated by the connections between corporate influence, provider conscience, and patient decision-making in Figure 5.2 above.) The federal Food, Drug, and Cosmetic Act (FDCA) authorizes the FDA to oversee DTC advertising to ensure that it is truthful, balanced, and accurate. Under the FDCA, the advertising for a drug, for example, must (1) not be false or misleading, (2) include specific disclosure about any serious risks associated with the drug, and (3) reveal its specific efficacy as it relates to specific population groups (e.g. the elderly, children) (FDCA, 21 USC 353b(b)–(e)).

Unlike the standards that govern corporate advertising, provider conscience finds itself between a rock and a hard place based on the expressed wants of a patient and the required disclosures under state informed consent laws. The principle of informed consent recognizes the autonomy of patients to be involved in decision-making affecting their health and well-being. It is therefore a right distinct from, although related to, patient decision-making as it is afforded by law with third party (i.e. provider) liability in the event of a violation thereof. In Illinois, for example, informed consent requires a disclosure of the procedure or service, and the attendant risks and benefits, along with its limitations and the meaning of results, as well as the patient's right to withdraw consent to the service at any time (e.g. 410 ILCS 305/3(2)). Patients thereby become participants in rather than objects of medical care.

Nonetheless, in the absence of strict disclosure vis-à-vis a mandatory vaccination law, which would require physicians to explicitly talk about the benefits and risks of vaccination, the impetus for vaccination may require initiation by the patient. Moreover, for socially controversial issues, some physicians may be reluctant to raise the issue outright. For example, one study found that many pediatricians did not discuss questions of sexuality unless asked for a specific explanation of a specific clinical problem (Esposito et al. 2007). Thus, patients who are uninformed or unaware of the potential benefits of a service will likely avoid it or be all the more reluctant to discuss it based on the information they have received.

In practice, patient decision-making is therefore influenced by factors independent of mere accessibility, cost, quality, and autonomy, which may explain existent trends in the uptake of particular services. Using a game theoretic-epidemiological model, we may explore how corporations, such as drug manufacturers, provide information (i.e. advertise) to providers (and perhaps patients) who, in turn, exercise their judgment to inform patients of particular services, including vaccines, screening, and testing.

V. Example: HPV Vaccination Uptake

We offer one example here to illustrate the general utility of the proposed model that utilizes a game theoretical-epidemiological framework, but at the same time we reiterate that the model is not topically-defined. The present inquiry on vaccination uptake is offered solely to demonstrate the precise impact of corporate influence and provider conscience and, consequently, the scope of legal issues that may be implicated.

The recently available vaccination to protect against human papillomavirus infection (HPV) has been shown to be effective as a clinical measure. At present over 20 million Americans are infected with HPV, with 6.2 million individuals becoming newly infected annually and an estimated 50% of all sexually active persons acquiring genital HPV at some point in their lives. In fact, over 25% of U.S. women aged 14 to 15 are infected with HPV, which can cause cervical cancer; though only 3.4% of U.S. women are infected with the strain of HPV that the new vaccine protects against. Consequently, the development of public policy and guidelines for administration of the vaccine has prompted significant public debate.

Physicians within an MLP must decide on whether to recommend vaccination uptake among male and female patients. The incentives to encourage vaccination are a *de facto* form of advertising that, notwithstanding the physician's motivations, will result in potential cost savings and revenue generation for the vaccine manufacturer (Merck) and the health system at large. In 2007 Merck spent over $100 million to advertise its HPV vaccine (Pettypiece 2007), and one report in a subsequent year estimated that $219 million of revenue was generated. Since our example is merely for the purpose of illustration, we shall estimate the advertising cost at $100 million with an attendant revenue generation of $219 million. For physicians, estimating how much advertising, i.e. enhanced physician-patient communication regarding the vaccine's benefits, would impact upon their revenue is far more elusive. We therefore suggest a cost of $5 million in lost revenue as a reasonable estimation, which is a fraction (5%) of what a major corporation like Merck would have to assume to reach its target population. The estimated savings for the health system have been calculated to be as low as $160 million in direct and indirect costs for prevention and treatment, with estimates ranging to over $4 billion (Hu and Goldie, 2008). Here, we assume the conservative figure of $160 million.

A. The Game and Rules

The proposed game is a multistage sequential-move advertising game whereby two players, Merck and all family medicine physicians, must decide to advertise the HPV vaccine to the target audience, which for purposes of this example will include all males and females aged 11 and older who are eligible for vaccination. The game begins with Merck having to decide whether to advertise or not, followed by physicians who, based upon Merck's decision to advertise (or not), must subsequently choose to advertise (i.e. recommend vaccination) to their patients.

The probabilities that we suggest for vaccination uptake are based on common sense assumptions that will find, irrespective of absolute values, that (1) the probability of vaccination will be highest (66%) among cohorts that are exposed to advertising by both Merck and physicians, which in turn (2) will be higher than uptake among cohorts who are subject to advertising by Merck but not physicians (5%), which in turn (3) will be higher than uptake among cohorts who are not subject to advertising by Merck, but are informed of the vaccine by physicians (3.5%), which in turn (4) will be higher than or equal to the uptake among a cohort that is not subject to any advertising (3.5%) whatsoever. It should be clear that the significant upsurge among individuals subject to both forms of advertising is consistent with the general effectiveness of advertising campaigns, and is the reason why corporations invest so heavily in advertising. Moreover, this is consistent with studies and anecdotal accounts by physicians who claim that many (if not most) of their patients learn about new drugs from DTC advertising vis-à-vis television and social media.

The payoffs were calculated by taking the sum of the cost (C5) and revenue (C5) and multiplying the product by the probability of vaccination (C6) to obtain the payoff of vaccination (C7). Here we are solely concerned with the decision to advertise based on the net positive payoff of vaccination. Still, the unrealized payoff due to non-vaccination is provided as the total revenue that could hypothetically be generated less the payoff of vaccination (C8). The payoffs are provided in the final column (C9), and include the payoff of each strategy, indicated by (Merck, Physicians). A summary chart of the strategies, players, costs, revenue, and payoffs are provided in Table 5.1.

A decision tree that outlines the sequential decision-making that begins with Merck's decision to advertise, followed by the physician's decision to recommend vaccination, is provided, along with the attendant probabilities of decisions and outcomes (i.e. vaccination), in Figure 5.3.

B. Brief Analysis

Suppose the doctors' strategy is to not advertise if Merck advertises, and also to not advertise if Merck does not advertise. Given this strategy, what is the best choice for Merck? If Merck chooses to advertise, it could earn $6 million since the physicians will not advertise (6, 8). If Merck chooses not to advertise, it will earn $8 million, since the doctors will not advertise (8, 6). Given a choice between earning $6 million and $8 million, Merck will prefer $8 million and will therefore choose not to advertise.

Table 5.1 Summary Chart of Strategies, Players, Costs, Revenue, and Payoffs

Strategy (C1)	Merck (C2)	Physicians (C3)	Cost (C4)	Revenue (C5)	Probability of Vaccination (C6)	Payoff of Vaccination (C7)=(C4+C5)*C6	(Unrealized payoff) C8=(Total (C5)- C7)	Payoffs (C9)
1	Advertise	Advertise	-100	219	0.66	79		79,102
			-5	160	0.66	102		
		Total		379		181	(198)	
2	Advertise	Don't Advertise	-100	219	0.05	6		6,8
			-5	160	0.05	8		
		Total		379		14	(365)	
3	Don't Advertise	Advertise	0	219	0.035	8		8,5
			-5	160	0.035	5		
		Total		379		13	(366)	
4	Don't Advertise	Don't Advertise	0	219	0.035	8		8,6
			0	160	0.035	6		
		Total		379		14	(365)	

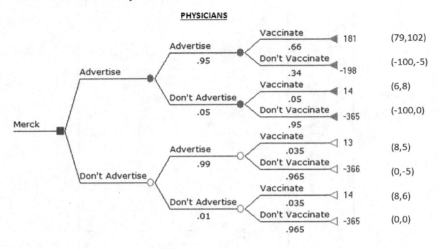

Figure 5.3 Decision Tree of Corporate Advertising and Provider Recommendation to Vaccinate

Given that Merck chooses not to advertise, do physicians have an incentive to change their strategy, i.e. to advertise? By choosing not to advertise if Merck does not advertise, physicians would earn $6 million, and if they choose to advertise, they would only earn $5 million (and note that Merck would still make the same amount of revenue at $8 million). We thus see that physicians have no incentive to change their strategy given that Merck chooses not to advertise. Since neither Merck nor the physicians have an incentive to change their strategies, we have a Nash equilibrium. The payoffs that result in this equilibrium are $8 million for Merck and $6 million for the physicians (8, 6).

Is this a reasonable outcome? Notice that the highest payoff for Merck results when Merck chooses to advertise and physicians choose to advertise as well. Why wouldn't Merck choose to advertise? Simply because the physicians threatened not to advertise if Merck chose to do so. If Merck chooses to advertise the physicians' best choice is to advertise, because the payoff would be $102 million compared to $8 million; if the physicians choose to advertise, Merck would make $79 million, which is higher than the payoff we estimated in the Nash equilibrium that we identified earlier.

Consequently, there is another Nash equilibrium in this game. Let's suppose the physicians' strategy is to choose to advertise if Merck chooses to advertise, but to choose not to advertise if Merck does not advertise. Given this strategy for the physicians, Merck earns $79 million by choosing to advertise, and $7 million by choosing not to advertise. In this scenario Merck would clearly choose to advertise, given the significant disparity in payoffs. Given that Merck will choose to advertise, the physicians have no incentive to change their strategy and we have another Nash equilibrium. Here, Merck earns $79 million and the physicians earn $102 million (79, 102).

We now must determine which of these two outcomes is more reasonable. Of the two Nash equilibriums that we have identified, the latter is more reasonable for the following reasons. In the first Nash equilibrium, Merck chooses not to advertise because the physicians threatened not to advertise if Merck chose to advertise. However, this threat is not credible and Merck would recognize as much. If this occurred, the physicians would have an incentive to change their strategies since choosing not to advertise after Merck has advertised would result in the physicians obtaining a significantly lower payoff ($8 million compared to $103 million). In other words, the physicians would have no incentive to do what they originally proclaimed as what they would intend to do. That is, the Nash equilibrium identified when neither Merck nor the physicians advertised is not a subgame perfect equilibrium. In this game, the only subgame perfect equilibrium is when Merck chooses to advertise and the physicians choose to advertise when Merck chooses to advertise (efficiency estimated at 100%).

VI. Outstanding Issues

This brief illustration of utilizing a game theoretic-epidemiological model provides an explanation of corporate and provider *incentives* that may, or may not, comport with actual practices. Moreover, we have not ascertained whether the translation of incentives into corporate advertising and physician conveyance of information were compliant with current standards of federal DTC laws and state informed consent laws, respectively. Consequently, our analysis of health law and management can be enriched—but certainly not supplanted—by integrating game theory, and epidemiology, into a broader framework to determine the nature and scope of federal and state statutes and regulations that impact upon the corporate-provider-patient relationship to secure individual and population health.

VII. Summary

The success of using a game theoretic-epidemiological model to inform a robust analysis of health law and management requires accurate estimations of probabilities and outcomes. These projects may employ surveys of providers and patients in an effort to secure those estimations, allowing for a meaningful interpretation of federal law as relates to corporate DTC and provider advertising; provider compliance with informed consent laws in the context of advertising and free speech; and patient interpretation of information received from both corporations and providers as indicated by subsequent decisions to avail themselves of particular healthcare services. At the very least, corporate influence and provider conscience should be included among the core focal points of public health policy to secure individual and population health and well-being.

References

AIDS Confidentiality Act of Illinois. 410 ILCS 305/3 et seq.

CDC. 2013. Human Papillomavirus Vaccination Coverage among Adolescent Girls, 2007–2012. *MMWR* 62(29):591–595.

Centers for Disease Control and Prevention (CDC). 2012. Genital HPV Infection Fact Sheet. August. http://www.cdc.gov/STD/HPV/STDFact-HPV.htm

Esposito S. et al. 2007. Pediatrician Knowledge and Attitudes Regarding Human Papillomavirus Disease and Its Prevention. *Vaccine* 25(35): 6437–6446.

Food and Drug Administration (FDA). 2004. The Impact of Direct-to-Consumer Advertising.   http://www.fda.gov/Drugs/ResourcesForYou/Consumers/ucm1 43562.htm

Food, Drug, and Cosmetic Act (FDCA). 21 USC 353b et seq.

Hall, M.A. 2006. The History and Future of Health Care Law: An Essentialist View. *Wake Forest Law Review* 41: 347–364.

Hu D. and S.J. Goldie. 2009. The Economic Burden of Noncervical Cancer Human Papillomavirus Disease in the United States. *Am J Obstet Gynecol* 198(5): 500.e1–500.e7.

Marmot, M.G. and R. G. Wilkerson (editors). 2006. *Social Determinants of Health*. 2nd edition. Oxford: Oxford University Press.

Pettypiece S. 2007. *Merck Aims Gardasil to Women Least Likely to Benefit*. Bloomberg.   http://www.bloomberg.com/apps/news?pid=newsarchive&sid=a m85Fd2sVycU

Part III

Social Determinants and Population Health

Innovation and Investment

6 Understanding How Health Happens

Your Zip Code is More Important Than Your Genetic Code

Anthony Iton, MD, JD, MPH and
Robert K. Ross, MD

I. Introduction

The Evergreen Jogging Track in Boyle Heights is a heavily frequented place for walkers, joggers, and moms pushing baby strollers. Working class Boyle Heights is not a place of many fancy health clubs or golf courses; it is a densely populated urban neighborhood sandwiched between multiple notorious LA freeways. The Evergreen Jogging Track is a place where all walks of East LA life come together to take advantage of vehicle-free exercise and the verdant ambiance. It is, in essence, an outdoor public health club. Over the years so many people used the path for their daily exercise over the years that neighborhood activists forced the city to install decorative streetlamps and a high-tech rubberized track surface so that residents could safely exercise without tripping over broken concrete and tree roots.

Throughout the United States there are "immigrant gateways"— communities that present new immigrants with their first taste of what America has to offer. Boyle Heights is one of those gateway communities. In the middle part of the last century in Los Angeles, Boyle Heights welcomed Jews, Latinos, Russians, African-Americans, Chinese, Portuguese, Armenians, Serbs, Croatians, and Japanese among others. When these groups acquired some money they often moved out of Boyle Heights to other parts of LA, making way for a new wave of immigrants. Boyle Heights today remains a working class, mostly Latino neighborhood east of downtown Los Angeles adjacent to the Los Angeles River.

An aerial view of Boyle Heights reveals multiple freeways, the 101, the I-5, the I-10, and a tight grid of city streets lined with the homes of the neighborhood's 90,000-plus residents. The sea of rooftops and concrete is only sporadically punctuated by green. Despite its dense population, Boyle Heights is park poor. According to the Los Angeles Department of City Planning, Boyle Heights has approximately 0.9 acres of park space per 1,000 residents, while the average in the City of Los Angeles is 8.9 acres per 1,000 residents—*almost 10 times as much!* There is a clear connection between easy access to parks and a person's health. People living near parks have greater opportunities to be physically active and lead active lifestyles that reduce stress and obesity, and even lower the risks of heart disease and diabetes. High-quality parks spur economic development by attracting homebuyers and boosting property values by as much as 15%. Exposure to the outdoors improves analytical thinking, making students better problem-solvers in math and science. Well-maintained parks promote community engagement and civic pride—many a community leader is born through efforts to improve local parks. There is less crime in residential areas close to parks. The list could go on, but the point is clear: parks result in stronger and safer communities.

Visible on the aerial map of Boyle Heights is Evergreen Cemetery, a big splotch of brownish-green. It is the biggest "greenspace" in Boyle Heights. Evergreen's tombstones mark the lives of Chinese laborers, black politicians, white land barons, Latino community leaders, and various successive waves of diverse immigrants. Yes, the Evergreen Jogging Track is built around a cemetery. It is hard not to see the cruel irony—residents striving to beat the odds and live long and healthy lives, running circles around tombstones coldly marking the shortened life expectancies of Boyle Heights residents.

Boyle Heights is also home to Hollenbeck Park, a beautiful century-old park. In 1960 it was violently transected by the I-5 freeway, with concrete freeway pylons plunked right down in the park's beautiful duck lagoon.

Figure 6.1 Aerial Map of Boyle Heights

Despite the noise and pollution, children and families determined to run free defy the signs that read "No soccer". They have no other choice. In Boyle Heights, there is literally nowhere else to play, except perhaps among the dead.

In 2010 the California Endowment initiated Building Healthy Communities (BHC), a ten-year, $1 billion health improvement initiative in Boyle Heights and thirteen other similarly situated neighborhoods throughout California where young children and families are struggling to find basic health opportunities like parks, grocery stores, and bike lanes. BHC is designed to remedy some of the glaring ironies found in Boyle Heights and throughout the state that create health disparities and ultimately rob low-income Californians of years of life.

II. From Health Disparities To Health Inequity

Just five miles to the west of Boyle Heights, down Cesar Chavez Avenue as it becomes Sunset Boulevard, is the community of Beverly Hills. If you live in Beverly Hills, you make more than twelve times the per capita income of residents who live in Boyle Heights. You also live six years longer (Health Atlas 2013). Recent studies show that the longevity gap between those with low and high income has been increasing dramatically in the US (Brookings 2016). Childhood obesity rates are also 2.5 times higher in Boyle Heights than in Beverly Hills. Boyle Heights is certainly not alone; many low income neighborhoods across the United States are plagued by profound health disparities. Beginning in 2008, a series of authoritative reports appeared in the scientific literature that summarized the astounding lack of progress in reducing health disparities in the U.S. According to the CDC, during the past decade, documented disparities have persisted for approximately 80% of the *Healthy People 2010* objectives and have increased for an additional 13% of the objectives (Myers, Yoon, and Kaufmann 2013). In its November 2015 report, *HHS Action Plan to Reduce Racial and Ethnic Health Disparities*, HHS notes that "[M]any leading health indicators, such as those from the Healthy People 2010 Final Review and the Agency for Healthcare Research and Quality (AHRQ) National Healthcare Disparities Report, have shown little reduction in racial and ethnic health disparities over the past decade" (U.S. Department of Health and Human Services 2015).

For many years the NIH promulgated a particularly unhelpful definition of health disparities that offered no insight regarding the social roots of health disparities: "Differences in the incidence, prevalence, mortality and burden of diseases and other adverse health conditions *that exist* among specific population groups in the United States" [emphasis added]. However, after the series of embarrassing reports documenting the lack of substantial progress in reducing U.S. health disparities, national public health leaders finally began to discard the somewhat simplistic notion of health disparities in favor of the concept of health inequity. Health inequities are disparities in health that are a result of systemic, avoidable, and unjust social and economic policies and practices that create barriers to opportunity. In their national reports on health disparities, HHS is now comfortable stating that: "Individuals, families and communities that have systematically experienced social and economic disadvantage face greater obstacles to optimal health. Characteristics such as race or ethnicity, religion, SES, gender, age, mental health, disability, sexual orientation or gender identity, geographic location, or other characteristics historically linked to exclusion or discrimination are known to influence health status" (U.S. Department of Health and Human Services 2015). The concept of health inequity acknowledges that life circumstances are not equal in the U.S. and that those unequal circumstances include neighborhood environments that are harsh, dangerous, and unhealthy, particularly if you are poor, black, Native American, or an immigrant.

A. Why Place?

A recent study of life expectancy in California demonstrated a twenty-five-year life expectancy gap between California neighborhoods (Woolf et al. in press). In the community with the lowest life expectancy in California residents can expect to live to about the age of 65, equivalent to the overall United States life expectancy in 1940. People in that California neighborhood are experiencing living conditions—in terms of both material and opportunity deprivation—that are about seventy-five years behind those of the average American, or about the equivalent of the country of Yemen. Residents of the California community at the top of the list can expect to live to almost 90 years old, longer than any country in the world. Two and a half decades of life separate the top of the list from the bottom in California. Why? Because our country was built on profound and pathological racial and class exploitation.

B. The Enduring Legacy of American Apartheid

Eight thousand. That is the number of children in Flint, Michigan that pediatrician Dr. Hanna-Attisha believes have been lead poisoned after the Michigan Governor's appointed Emergency Manager switched drinking water sources for the City of Flint (Goodnough 2016). Lead is an irreversible neurotoxin to children, impairing their IQ and behavior.

Historically, redlining practices consigned African Americans to Flint's north end where today many homes sit abandoned, essentially worthless, in the shadow of enormous and defunct auto plants. Over the past several decades Flint's population plummeted by half after auto plants shut down, rapid disinvestment set in, and massive white flight reshaped the city's demographics. African Americans now make up 57% of Flint's population, and 40% of Flint's residents live below the poverty line. Marginalized, devalued, and ignored, the basic human needs of Flint's mostly black and poor residents were barely even an afterthought when Flint's Emergency Manager decided to switch the city's drinking water to the notoriously murky Flint River.

As in Michigan and elsewhere in the United States, our neighborhoods in California did not evolve naturally. The practice of geographically separating people into different neighborhoods according to race, income, religion, and ethnicity is a longstanding practice in the United States. For the majority of the twentieth century these segregation practices were sanctioned by local, state, and federal governments (McKibben 2011; Self 2003). This practice is so embedded in our culture that we have numerous colloquial terms for undesirable neighborhoods: ghetto, barrio, slum, reservation, trailer park, and of course, "wrong side of the tracks". When speaking about desirable neighborhoods we speak of upscale, well-to-do, affluent, exclusive, or posh. We do not hesitate to use these terms in everyday conversation, almost as if this is just a natural phenomenon, but the reality is that we have been actively shaping and reshaping neighborhoods through policy (redlining, racially-restrictive covenants, steering, zoning, subprime lending) for over one hundred years in California (Self 2003).

Of course, associated with neighborhood type is the quality of schools, parks, stores, transportation systems, housing, infrastructure, and even street quality and design. These neighborhood amenities and resources have been conclusively linked to health status. So why is it that we are surprised by expectancy differences of two and a half decades between neighborhoods? We have literally designed this health outcome into our land use decision making. This wide spectrum of life expectancy is patterned into the wide spectrum of neighborhood environments that we have designed and reinforced through land use policy—so much so that we can say *"when it comes to your health, your zip code is more important than your genetic code"*. Or better still, *"Give me your address, and I'll tell you how long you'll live"*.

Growing up on the "wrong side of the tracks" is a familiar part of the American narrative. Many great leaders, artists, athletes, and entertainers describe an origin story that is set in a ghetto fraught with hazards and risk. Their rags-to-riches stories never fail to captivate and intrigue us and make up the very essence of the American Dream. But the truth is, these stories wouldn't stand out if more of their peers and friends could actually "make it out". Economic and social mobility has declined in this country (Chetty 2014), so millions of low-income Californians are consigned to the same stark neighborhood conditions for much of their lives. While many do move, more often than not they move to communities with the same basic socio-economic status and thus similar neighborhood conditions. Low income people and people of color disproportionately reside in communities that are systematically deprived of critical health protective resources such as parks, grocery stores, good schools, quality housing, and maybe most importantly, hope.

C. Rich People and Poor People Are Physiologically Different

Like all Californians, low-income people are in search of opportunity. They seek safe places to raise their children with good schools, clean parks, healthy food, good transportation, and decent and affordable housing. However, because many low income neighborhoods lack these basic resources, low-income Californians are often shrouded in a fog of chronic stress that results from having to navigate multiple daily hazards including crime, traffic, poor quality housing, and low quality schools. Many of us have to balance some risks against our resources. If you think of risks as juggling balls, we juggle a couple of balls every day. However, if you are on a low income, you are constantly forced to juggle multiple balls and inevitably balls get dropped. When higher income people drop balls they have resources (e.g. savings, employers, banks, home equity, healthcare) that will help them respond to the consequences of dropping a ball. When low income people drop one of their many balls, the consequences are more severe (e.g. foreclosure, eviction, homelessness, untreated illness). The constant worry that results from having to juggle so many balls produces chronic stress that actually changes our physiology. Chronic stress kills. It kills by altering our physiology to exacerbate cardiovascular injury, accelerate chronic disease, and facilitate premature aging (MacArthur Research Network). Chronic stress also changes how our brains function and limits executive function—the ability to plan, focus attention, remember instructions, and juggle multiple tasks successfully (Harvard Center). As a consequence, poor people are physically different from rich people. Residents of low-income communities are forced to contend with high levels of chronic stress due to a lack of control of the multiple stressors that confront them on a daily basis. Poverty robs people of control over their lives. That lack of control, or agency, steadily erodes health and fosters a pervasive sense of hopelessness in many low-income communities. Much of this is unnecessary and the product of inequitable American policy, or often times it is the inevitable product of the absence of appropriate policy in the face of abject need.

III. The Bay Area Regional Health Inequities Initiative

In 2002 a group of public health officials in the San Francisco Bay Area came together out of frustration that the tools of the traditional "medical model" approach to public health practice were not sufficient for the challenges facing modern public health. Chief among those challenges was health inequity. Recognizing that health outcomes are strongly influenced by the social and environmental conditions that many low-income people in the Bay Area are forced to contend with on a daily basis, these pioneering health officials created the Bay Area Regional Health Inequities Initiative (BARHII) whose mission is to transform public health practice with the purpose of eliminating health inequities, using a broad spectrum of approaches that create healthy communities (www.barhii.org). The BARHII framework is an effort to visualize and organize public health interventions and strategies across a spectrum from downstream to upstream. In essence, the BARHII framework is an integration of the medical model and the socio-ecological model with a specific eye towards situating types of interventions along the upstream-downstream continuum.

The basic idea underlying the BARHII framework is that upstream inequity creates downstream disparity. The medical model focuses on preventing premature death by treating and managing disease and injury that is the product of risk factors and risk behaviors like smoking, poor diet, and lack of exercise. The medical model is grounded in the assumption that autonomous individuals are making independent behavioral choices from a broad array of options, some healthy and others not. The tools of the medical model are healthcare services, health education, and to a limited extent, genetic analysis and modification. The medical model costs $3 trillion per year ($9523 per capita) or 17.5% of the gross domestic product. Meanwhile upstream, the socio-ecological model recognizes that

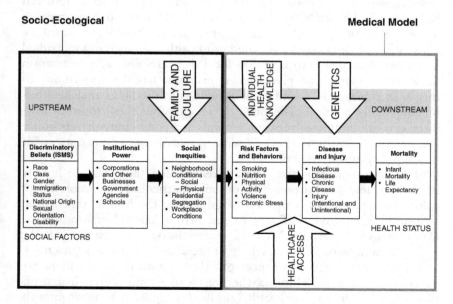

Figure 6.2 A Framework for Health Equity

social inequities (e.g. inner cities, barrios, and reservations) are the product of past and current policy (redlining, racially restrictive covenants, and housing policy) that ultimately derives from a narrative that values different people differently as a result of a set of well entrenched "isms". A simple example is how a narrative of racism produces policies like racial segregation that lead directly to inner cities, a stark and outrageous social inequity. The BARHII framework acknowledges that within the medical model we have defined interventions for each of the boxes: emergency rooms to prevent death, clinical care to treat and manage disease, and health education to help change behaviors. However, within public health practice, we have no organized interventions to improve neighborhood conditions, change unhealthy policies, or change the overarching narrative about health.

At the California Endowment we have translated the upstream elements of the BARHII framework into a public health practice focused on improving community environments by changing policies and systems and re-shaping the narrative and power structures that influence those policies.

IV. Building Healthy Communities

Building Healthy Communities (BHC) is a holistic attempt to help reweave the fraying fabric of low-income communities by harnessing the latent power and potential of their residents. It is a ten-year, $1 billion, place-based initiative, launched in 2010, that aims to transform fourteen communities by building *power* (social, political, and economic), implementing proven health protective *policy*, and changing the *narrative* about what produces health (beyond just health insurance and individual behavior). The idea is to revitalize local democracy so as to transform these environments into places where everyone has the opportunity to thrive. In short, BHC's strategy is grounded in the belief that health is fundamentally political. The BHC model envisions these fourteen low-income communities as proving grounds for community-driven policy and practice innovations that will serve to inform and advance statewide health policy and systems change.

BHC is grounded in the sobering reality that the odds are heavily stacked against low income Californians, particularly communities of color. To achieve TCE's mission of improving the health status of all Californians, it is not sufficient to just help a handful of low income Californians beat the odds. We must change the odds. Consistent with the BARHII framework, due to a legacy of racial and economic segregation, anti-immigrant policy and a host of other historical "isms', there are many communities in California where residents are mired in environments that conspire to injure their health. Like Boyle Heights, these environments lack basic health protective amenities like parks, grocery stores, decent schools, functioning transportation systems, affordable and decent housing, living wage jobs, and even potable water in some instances. These same environments concentrate risk such as liquor stores, fast food, payday lenders, environmental pollution, and crime. In these environments, community residents are forced to constantly navigate multiple risks without the benefit of significant resources.

These neighborhood and community environments are not natural, they are manmade, and they can be unmade. Building Healthy Communities is an effort that enlists the very residents who have been the targets of exclusion, stigma, and discrimination in remaking their environments through holding local, regional, and state systems accountable for creating healthy and equitable community environments.

The BHC theory of change is about building community capacity (increasing social, political, and economic power and changing the narrative about health), to change policy and systems, in order to create healthy environments that will (over time) improve health status. The targeted policy and systems change is multi-level: local, regional, and statewide. BHC is particularly focused on improving the social and health outcomes of populations that have been under threat, such as Boys and Men of Color (BMOC), immigrants, LGBTQ, and formerly incarcerated individuals, and consequently BHC has a special focus on strategies that enhance opportunity structures for these populations.

BHC operates by creating unprecedented space for community organizing, leadership development, and sustained multi-sector collaboration by enabling residents, community groups, and institutional leaders to collaborate across all sorts of boundaries, such as race, ethnicity, age, as well as the boundary that can exist between local communities and external professionals. Across all fourteen sites, the approach focuses on five drivers that we believe are necessary for propelling the priorities forward: building people power, youth leadership development, multi-sector collaboration and policy innovation, leveraging resources and partnerships, and changing the narrative.

Figure 6.3 Building Healthy Communities: A Theory of Change

While the approach is the same across all of the sites, how it manifests depends on the local circumstances. In Fresno, for instance, the work is taking the form of unlikely alliances between community and environmental groups all interested in ensuring the city grows sustainably, whether for the people who live there or the environment. In East Salinas, the community is coming together with public servants to transform the way the city governs so that racial equity is at the forefront of all policies, practices, and procedures. While a significant portion of the plan involves "place-based" attention in fourteen communities across the state, of equal importance is how the reality tested the strategy; the collective learning and energy from these communities contribute to statewide policy and systems change to promote health, health equity, and health justice for all Californians. BHC is a place-based strategy, but with an orientation toward statewide change – we call it "place-based-plus".

V. Defining BHC Success

How are we defining "success" for BHC? For us, the key BHC goals will not be limited to an arbitrary ten-year timeline. They will be achieved when three things happen to benefit the health of young people in low-income communities in California:

- 100% coverage and access to health-promoting and prevention-focused health services
- 100% of California's schools with wellness and school climate policies and practices designed to enhance the social and emotional health of all children
- 100% of California's cities and counties establishing health-promoting policies, particularly in youth development, land-use, and criminal justice

The thinking behind these three targets for policy and systemic change is that the wellness of young people is optimized when the primary "systems" they encounter—the health and social service systems, the school, and the neighborhood—are supporting what families want for their children's health and well-being. True success, however, will come when the power dynamics in the communities have shifted to such an extent that families are able to hold local officials accountable for full, ongoing implementation of these policies. Healthy communities are inclusive, democratic, and allow all community members to participate.

A. What Has Been Achieved To Date?

Ascribing positive impact to a specific grant, a set of grants, or a grant making strategy is fraught with important issues of "attribution" vs.

"contribution". BHC works in deep and extensive partnership with organized community residents, advocacy groups, service providers, media, and policy-makers. The successes described below are shared successes to which BHC has contributed. That said, the extent and timelines of many of these wins would likely not have been possible but for BHC. The following is a top-line listing of key results where BHC grantees, with TCE in partnership support, have made a significant contribution towards impact. Perhaps most importantly, each of these provides powerful evidence of deep community transformation. These achievements would not have been accomplished without the bravery of traditionally marginalized residents leading waves of change.

1. Improved Health Coverage for the Underserved

BHC grantees and partners fought for and supported the successful implementation of the Affordable Care Act and the expansion of Medicaid in California. Due to these efforts, there are more than four million new Medi-Cal enrollees since 2010.

2. Strengthened Health Coverage Policy for the Undocumented

BHC grantees and partners successfully crafted and led the Health 4 All Campaign, paving the way for state-supported health coverage for undocumented children and preserving county-level health access for undocumented adults. 250,000 children are newly eligible for coverage, and thousands of undocumented adults maintain access to healthcare.

3. School Climate, Wellness and Equity Improvements

Local BHC youth identified school discipline as a priority issue. Local and statewide BHC grantees, partners, along with youth, led or supported efforts across the state to reform harsh school discipline and suspension policies, and are working to successfully implement school equity funding formulas. School suspensions are down by 40% since 2009–10.

4. Local and Regional Progress: Health in all Policies

The physical, social, and political environments in BHC communities are being transformed by the work of residents that are advocating, innovating, and crafting new local policies and system changes that promote a strong culture of "health in all policies". More than one hundred new policies, including those that foster more walkable communities, fresh food access, park space, and access to clean drinking water, have been adopted.

5. Public-Private Investment and Policy Changes for Boys and Young Men of Color

BHC grantees joined with other coalitions supporting outcomes improvement work among young men of color, bringing improved public policy and civic attention to the issue, and resulting in the creation of a Boys and Young Men of Color Select Committee in the state legislature.

6. Prevention and Reform Support in the Justice System

BHC grantees and partners led advocacy support for health- and prevention-oriented justice reform, and are leading Prop 47 implementation efforts statewide and locally; one of the key objectives is to funnel prison savings into prevention strategies. One million Californians are eligible for reclassification.

VI. What Has Been Learned?

We commissioned independent reviews of our progress from three respected entities: FSG; the University of Southern California PERE Center; and the Center on Effective Philanthropy (CEP). (To be precise, we were approached by CEP as part of their "Philamplify" initiative, and agreed to cooperate with their assessment tool on social change philanthropy.)

The three reports were generally consistent in their findings. In addition to describing significant levels of activity in each of the BHC communities, they also pointed out the challenges inherent in such a complex undertaking, such as maintaining clarity regarding operational priorities and the alignment of understanding and effort across all the diverse participants in the enterprise.

Through our experience in BHC, we have learned a great deal about how to capitalize on key policy developments—some anticipated, others not—affecting our communities, such as the implementation of the Affordable Care Act (ACA), the advent of the Local School Funding Formula, and upheavals in immigration policy such as DACA. Along the way, BHC has grown into a dynamic, continuously evolving hybrid of locally driven work and state-level policy campaigns. That makes it a particularly challenging entity to evaluate in simple terms.

We also have some feedback from our grantees through the Center for Effective Philanthropy survey, where we learned that our strengths lie in the realm of public policy and policy change, but we need to improve in grantee relations. Finally, an internal survey of program staff revealed a consensus desire to build on BHC's developed strengths and community capacity to drive systemic change in service of healthier communities.

A. Overall, we learned the following about our progress:

- The top-line lesson for us has been a crystal-clear affirmation about the importance of leaders in underserved and low-income communities wielding the civic and political power required to effect health-promoting systems change. For all of the attention heaped upon the importance of "good data", "research effectiveness", and "innovative approaches" to drive public policy, the building of healthier communities is fundamentally a game about power, voice, and advocacy. Plugging the voice of community into the right kind of political power grid will do more to create health and wellness than any other single intervention.

- Our "theory of change" to help communities and health advocates assert power in economically challenged communities actually works. We have invested a substantial amount of grant dollars funding key "Drivers of Change" for grantees at the state and local levels: People Power, Youth Leadership, Collaboration, Partnerships, and Narrative Change. Community engagement has ranged from solid to excellent across the BHC spectrum, levels of trust between communities and our foundation are improving, and we have some local and statewide results to show for it.

- Local BHC and statewide campaigns have taken off. Locally, residents and leaders have led efforts to shape "health in all policies" approaches, scoring more than one hundred victories across the sites in land use planning and walkable communities, healthy eating and wellness policies in schools, public health emphases in municipal and county General Plans, and new skate parks, soccer fields, and after school programs for children and youth. Institutionally, we have developed a sharper understanding about the role a private foundation can play in supporting a community-driven and community-engaged campaign.

- On the statewide front, local BHC residents and youth leaders joined hands to advance healthier school climate policies, educate and enroll uninsured residents into the ACA and Medicaid expansion opportunities (we are proud to have contributed to California's success in ACA and Medicaid expansion enrollment), successfully advocate for undocumented residents to have access to healthcare, and push for more prevention-oriented law enforcement and criminal justice reforms.

- All fourteen BCH sites have experienced progress at varying levels. Early struggles experienced in several sites were managed through a combination of patience, improved communications, candor, and trust-building. Any fears experienced about needing to "drop" any troubled sites have been discarded. As a result, we are now trusted across the sites to stay the course and not flee at the first sign of difficulty. Our approach works in both heavily urban and under resourced rural sites.

- Youth engagement in and across the fourteen sites has been a particular strong point. All sites have young people meaningfully engaged at the table, and youth organizing to promote health is emerging as a signature hallmark of BHC. That said, we have also learned, through young people directly communicating their experiences—backed up by the data—that they, and their families, are coping with substantial levels of stress, adversity, and trauma in their daily lives. The depth of the issues of toxic stress, exposure to trauma, and resiliency in young people of color—and their collective effects on wellness—represents a major "discoverable" in the BHC journey. Based on the combination of the emerging science and the emerging voices of advocates for young people of color, exposure to trauma and stress is a substantially under-recognized public health crisis in this nation.

B. Creating Health Equity: A Story From Fresno BHC

Like Boyle Heights, South Fresno is park poor. Residents in South Fresno have one fourth as much park space as residents of wealthier North Fresno. Community residents in South Fresno came together through BHC to change that.

They studied the city's Master Plan and used the data in that plan to shine a light on the disparity between the wealthy and poor parts of town. They organized a campaign to get the City to commit to rectifying the clear park disparity and update the city's Master Plan. The Parks4All

Figure 6.4 Fresno Building Health Communities

campaign mobilized hundreds of South Fresno residents and youth. To raise the profile of this issue these organized residents began calling their City Council members, writing letters to the editors in the local press, holding press conferences, and attending City Council meetings. They did extensive research and polled the community. They found that more than two-thirds of all Fresnans wanted more parks and recreation services for youth and greater funding for the Parks and Recreation Department. They designed and displayed billboards, bus shelter ads, and newspaper ads. Soon newspaper editorial boards began editorializing in support and political cartoons were published mocking the Mayor and the City Council for their intransigence. In September 2015, after months of concerted advocacy from South Fresno residents, the Fresno City Council voted unanimously to allocate $450,000 to update Fresno's twenty-six-year-old Parks Master Plan. This success was driven by low-income young people and their families in South Fresno.

VII. Our BHC Strategy Moving Forward: Building on Progress

Based on our experience and the voices of resident and youth leaders across our fourteen BHC sites, the complex matter of 'health equity for all' cannot be achieved unless: 1) we build on the health coverage success of the ACA to undertake health reform 2.0, which involves moving dollar expenditures from outrageously costly back-end care, upstream into new and expanded wellness/ prevention/population health funding streams; 2) health and public health leaders join forces with advocates and activists to dismantle the incarceration superhighway and move incarceration dollars into behavioral health treatment and jobs; 3) health system leaders, health workforce/health professions schools and schools of public health reimagine training with communities and population health at the center of a more prevention-minded health system; 4) local and state political and civic leaders come to grips with the reality that meaningful civic engagement and civic participation is good for the nation's health, and exclusion and marginalization is lethal; and 5) local, state and national philanthropy must be more assertive in the recognition of the relationship between political power and health outcomes, and be more willing to fund advocacy, civic engagement, and power-building at the level of community.

A. Key Lessons For Designing A Health Equity Practice

Health equity requires us to ask the simple question: How did we get here? It is impossible to move forward to correct health inequity if we do not understand how we created it. Our history reveals how we have discriminated against poor people and people of color in California in ways that impair health for generation after generation. This discrimination was mediated through policy and politics. In 2016 we are still repairing the damage of those decisions, while struggling against efforts that would do further damage. So in that way we recognize that health is political. One definition of politics is "the struggle over the allocation of scarce and precious social goods". When it comes to community health, these scarce and precious social goods may be a park or a grocery store. In the process of implementing BHC, we have noticed many salutary benefits of helping communities to develop their social, political, and economic power. An important recognition is that power, or agency, is good for your health. Both individual agency and collective agency have salutary health benefits, particularly for young people.

Another emerging learning point is that discrimination injures people in ways beyond denying them resources. Discrimination and exclusion injure a person's sense of belonging and connectedness. When people feel isolated and disconnected from their community, their health suffers. When whole communities feel like they do not belong, there is a collective trauma that can have profound and intergenerational effects. One important strategy in helping heal that trauma is by organizing the very people who have been traumatized and enlisting them to help rebuild their communities by holding systems accountable for equity and restoring health and justice. Building Healthy Communities is one foundation's model for trying to build health equity. Over the next five years we plan to continue to build and refine this model.

References

Bay Area Regional Health Inequities Initiative. www.barhii.org

Brookings. 2016. *The Growing Gap in Longevity Between the Rich and Poor.* February 16. http://www.brookings.edu/research/podcasts/2016/02/rich-poor-life-expectancy-gap Accessed April 28, 2016.

Chetty, R. 2014. Is the United States Still a Land of Opportunity? Recent trends in intergenerational mobility. *American Economic Review Paper and Proceedings* 104(5): 141–147.

Goodnough, A. 2016. Flint weighs scope of harm to children caused by lead in water. *New York Times* January 29.

Harvard Center on the Developing Child. Executive Function and Self-Regulation. http://developingchild.harvard.edu/science/key-concepts/executive-function/ Accessed April 28, 2016.

Health Atlas for the City of Los Angeles. 2013. http://planning.lacity.org/cwd/framwk/healthwellness/text/healthatlas.pdf

MacArthur Research Network on SES & Health. http://www.macses.ucsf.edu Accessed April 28, 2016.

McKibben, C.L. 2011. *Racial Beachhead: Diversity and Democracy in A Military Town.* Stanford, California: Stanford University Press.

Myers, P.A, P.W. Yoon, and R.B. Kaufmann. 2013. Introduction: CDC health disparities and inequalities report—United States. *Morbidity and Mortality*

Weekly Report. 62(03): 3–5 http://www.cdc.gov/mmwr/preview/mmwrhtml/su6203a2.htm Accessed April 28, 2016

Self, R.O. 2003. *American Babylon: Race and the Struggle for Postwar Oakland.* Princeton, NJ: Princeton University Press.

Terriquez, V. & I. Bloemrad. 2016. Cultures of Engagement: The organizational foundations of advancing health in immigrant and low-income communities of color. *Social Science and Medicine.* 165(September): 214–222.

U.S. Department of Health and Human Services. 2015. *HHS Action Plan to Reduce Racial and Ethnic Health Disparities: Implementation Progress Report 2011–2014.* Washington, DC: Office of the Assistant Secretary for Planning and Evaluation http://minorityhealth.hhs.gov/assets/pdf/FINAL_HHS_Action_Plan_Progress_Report_11_2_2015.pdf

Woolf, S. et al. *California Mortality Study* [in publication]

7 Designing Partnerships and Building Relationships

A Social Responsibility to Reduce African American Child Mortality

Chet P. Hewitt, JD

A just society is that society in which ascending sense of reverence and descending sense of contempt is dissolved into the creation of a compassionate society.

B.R. Ambedkar

I. Introduction

This chapter focuses on leadership practice in a case study of how the Sierra Health Foundation helped launch an effort to reduce disproportionate African American child mortality rates in an urban area of over one million residents in Sacramento County, California.

A starting point for understanding our approach to participating in this effort to reduce African American child mortality can be found in the foreword to *Introduction to Social Justice* that was written in 1948, by Norman Kurland. Kurland recounts the author's, Father William Ferree's, admonition that we have a moral duty to continually reorganize society for the common good as a consequence of our growing understanding of the concept of social responsibility—as opposed to individual responsibility—and, now knowing this, we all have a responsibility to work toward solving the disparities and social injustices that exist in the world. Ferree goes on to state that how well we advance social justice in turn can be measured for each institution in terms of that institution's success in evaluating the dignity, status, power, and well-being of every participating person and family it serves.

Ferree's statement provides a compelling moral justification for undertaking social justice work, and perhaps the ultimate set of measures for evaluating its success. The elegance and clarity in his writing transcends the years that have gone by since it was first published. In many ways, it captures the most relevant and powerful theme percolating within social welfare policy debates today—how to advance equity. While Ferree's comments allude to the importance of changing society's view of and response to those experiencing poverty, it does not offer guidance with respect to the characteristics and approaches leaders will need to adopt to achieve the lofty goal of a more just and equitable society. Specifically, the effort described in this case study is rooted in the promise of health equity and the essential role leadership and community empowerment strategies are playing in an ongoing effort to reduce disproportionate African American child death in Sacramento County.

II. Social Justice and Health Equity

Within healthcare today there is a growing recognition that some of the most challenging and widespread health challenges we face as a nation will require health and human service systems to think and work outside of their current boundaries. This reality makes the examination of leadership approaches that are attempting to engage community in health-oriented system change efforts valuable to our ability to effectively engage in this type of work going forward. Accordingly, my purpose here is to contribute to this conversation by writing about my experience co-leading an ongoing health equity/social determinants of health challenge that has at its center issues of race, place, class, and institutional change. Over time I hope to expand on this case study by discussing what has helped and hindered our efforts to reduce child death rates in Sacramento County, with the hope that the themes and approaches that surface will prove helpful to the efforts of other leaders working to advance health equity.

The Sierra Health Foundation: Center for Health Program Management's involvement in Sacramento County's effort to reduce disproportionate African American (AA) child mortality rates began shortly after the conclusion of a public process initiated by recently elected County Supervisor Phil Serna. Shortly after beginning his term of office in 2011, Supervisor Serna attended a board session in which Sacramento County's twentieth annual child death review report was presented. The Supervisor was deeply moved to learn of the high rate of mortality affecting AA children, and was compelled to act upon learning the disparate death rate had remained consistent for twenty consecutive years. Shortly after receiving the report, he persuaded his colleagues on the County Board to establish a Blue Ribbon Commission, which he chaired, to investigate the matter in greater detail. As president of the Sierra Health Foundation (SHF) and its independent affiliate, SHF: Center for Health Program Management (Center), I was asked and accepted an invitation from Supervisor Serna to serve as a member of the commission. To be clear, it was the courage and compassion of Supervisor Serna, who continues to serve as the effort's political champion, which paved the way for this work to begin.

Two years later the Center took on a formal role after the Commission issued its final report. The report contained several recommendations, including the establishment of a committee to implement the broader set of recommendations brought forth by the Commission. To this end the Sacramento County Board of Supervisors created the Committee to Reduce African American Child Death (RAACD) and mandated that its membership include faith-based, philanthropic and nonprofit leaders, children and family advocates, public institution representatives, and youth and community leaders from impacted communities. The report also recommended that the RAACD Committee should be provided with administrative support to ensure it had the capacity to pursue the mandate that led to its creation. The Sierra Health Foundation: Center for Health Program Management was privileged to be selected to serve as the Committee's administrative entity. The Center leadership enthusiastically sought out this role, believing that the RAACD Committee's mission aligned well with the purpose that gave rise to the Center's founding several years earlier.

The Center is an intermediary founded upon a number of core values: inclusion, diversity, community empowerment, and accountability. The intentional process that gave rise to its formation pushed the Center's board and leadership to think seriously about the rationale, purpose, and role of an intermediary. We came to the conclusion that working intentionally and deliberately across racial, ethnic, geographic, and historical divides of power and influence in order to facilitate transformational social change was an important contribution that we as an institution could make toward the creation of a more just and equitable society. From the perspective of mission, the Center would focus on Social Justice as its North Star goal, and organizationally to model collective impact as the pathway for facilitating change (Kania and Kramer, 2011). Programmatically, our strategy would focus on: health equity, or the absence of systematic disparities in health and well-being between groups with different levels of underlying social advantage or disadvantage—that is, wealth, power, or prestige (Braveman and Gruskin, 2003); and the social determinants of health as the conditions in which people are born, grow, work, live, and age, and the wider set of forces and systems shaping the conditions of daily life.

Our intermediary role calls on us to connect with, resource, and support disparate groups whose collaboration is essential to their ability to achieve a shared goal. Our experience has been that far too often groups that need to work together closely to succeed lack the requisite history, relationship, and credibility required to do so effectively. We believe that leading an intermediary requires an institutional base from which to connect with other institutions, and a willingness to invest in and view connection as a valued outcome. This is the reasoning behind our Foundation and operating Center model. Importantly, we accept and value our ability to invest in the leadership of others, and find purpose and accomplishment in our efforts to gauge how effectively we leverage our influence, networks, and resources in service to others.

III. Findings

Of California's fifty-eight counties, Sacramento is one of approximately twenty-two that have an active child death review program. The Sacramento County Child Death Review Team (CDRT) reviews the deaths of all children who die in Sacramento County, and reports its findings every two years to the County Board of Supervisors. CDRTs, generally, were established upon a simple and powerful premise: a comprehensive analysis of all child deaths in a given jurisdiction would enable child-serving institutions, elected officials, and other key stakeholders to prevent future child deaths. With this as their charge, for twenty years Sacramento's CDRT, which has been well managed by the Child Abuse and Prevention Council, has consistently reported that African American children died at a rate two times higher than children of other races.

From 1990 through 2009 there was a total of 3,633 Sacramento County resident child deaths, with a child defined as an individual of 0 to17 years of age. The overall child death rate over this time was 53.20 per 100,000 Sacramento County resident children. During this period, 816 Sacramento County African American resident children died, a rate of 102 per 100,000. Despite reductions in overall child mortality rates for all racial groups over this period, African American children consistently died at a disproportionate rate of twice that of other children. As reported in the Sacramento Blue Ribbon Commission on Child Death's report, of the 3,633 child deaths between 1990 and 2010, African American children accounted for 22% (816) of child deaths, while representing only 12% of the children. The report also identified the four causes of death that had the most disproportionate impact on African American children in Sacramento County. These were: third-party child homicides; infant sleep-related deaths; child abuse and neglect homicides; and perinatal condition deaths. Through geo-mapping, the report also identified six neighborhoods that accounted for 82% of all African American child deaths in these four categories. For many Sacramentans who followed the Commission's work, it was surprising to learn that *one third of all children who suffered infant sleep-related death during the twenty-year reporting period were African American.* However, it was not surprising for them to learn that the six most impacted communities were also some of the poorest neighborhoods in the County.

Upon completing its review, the Blue Ribbon Commission set a goal of reducing preventable causes of disproportionate African American child death by 10% to 20% over a five-year period. The Commission also proposed the adoption of six overarching recommendations, in addition to the creation of the RAACD, to guide future work. Summarized, these additional recommendations include:

Table 7.1 Greatest Disproportion of Child Deaths

Top Six Neighborhoods and Top Four Causes of Child Death with the Greatest Disproportion
Sacramento County Resident Child Deaths 1990–2009

	# AA Third-Party Child Homicide	# AA Infant Sleep-Related Deaths	# AA CAN Homicides	# AA Perinatal Death	# Total AA Deaths Among Four Categories	# Total Deaths in All Races Among Four Categories	AA Child Deaths as % of All Child Deaths Among Four Categories	AA Children as % Total Child Population in Each Neighborhood
Meadowview/Valley Hill	19	32	15	116	182	446	41	16
Arden-Arcade	1	6	7	19	33	95	35	8
North Sacramento/Del Paso Heights	9	17	3	34	63	212	30	16
Oak Park	1	7	4	11	23	84	27	9
North Highlands/Foothill	5	11	7	22	45	188	24	9
Fruitridge/Stockton Blvd.	4	11	6	25	46	194	24	8

- Deliberately consider the interest and well-being of all children
- Collaborate with other initiatives working to address determinants of health that impact disparities in the African American community
- Support existing efforts to reduce disproportionate African American child deaths
- Engage and empower members of the African American community to help implement, inform, and advocate for culturally appropriate strategies
- Launch a coordinated community education and prevention campaign to address the top four causes of disproportionate child death in the African American community
- Improve data collection and data sharing across systems to access critical information and monitor change

In June 2013 the Reduction of African American Child Deaths committee was established by resolution of the Sacramento County Board of Supervisors. Funded by Sacramento County and First 5 Sacramento and managed by the Sierra Health Foundation: Center for Health Program Management, the twenty-five-member Committee includes representatives from county agencies, education, health systems, civic groups, faith-based organizations, community parents and youth groups, and policy advocates. The RAACD officially began its work in the fall of 2013.

IV. Lesson Learned

A. Leadership Matters

As the RAACD Committee effort got underway, the first course of action was to select its leadership. At a meeting convened by Supervisor Serna to launch the Committee he asked the group to select its leadership rather than have him select it for them. He cautioned the group to take seriously its first decision, making clear his feelings that the effort needed effective leadership in order to sustain the tenuous political support that had allowed it to advance to this point. He reiterated that going forward an actionable plan, both meeting the specific requirements articulated in the Blue Ribbon Commission report and inspiring confidence on the part of the Board, had to be presented or the plan would not be funded. In one thoughtful move, the modeling of shared leadership had begun.

As expected within a group of well-regarded individuals, several members wanted to lead the effort. As the meeting progressed, a proposal was presented that promoted the idea of the group selecting a non-typical, less experienced member as the best way to proceed. Several of us in the room, including myself, who were experienced health, human service and community leaders knew this was a statement targeted at us. The statement seemed to resonate within the group and after a fair amount of conversation and several rounds of voting a less experienced chairperson was selected. Myself and a deeply committed community activist, also less experienced, became finalists for the position of vice-chair. The activist, in part responding to the earlier statement about selection, said that if I wanted the position she would withdraw her name. As the group looked to see my reaction, I did what I thought best and ceded the opportunity to the grass roots advocate. Looking back, I consider this the second expression of modeling shared leadership, both of which would turn out to be important moments in the early part of our journey. What is important here is not Supervisor Serna's approach or my individual act, but rather the notion of servant leadership as a model for sharing authority and building trust, even when the opportunity doesn't require that you do so. In that moment, we demonstrated leadership by being willing to follow. I believe this was an important learning opportunity for our group as we worked to set a benchmark for the type of leadership model we would employ going forward.

Unfortunately, the effort began to falter as meetings were not managed well and timelines were missed. Doubt began to replace the promise and hope the Committee had possessed when it began its works. The lack of progress began to cause tension among Committee members, who increasingly felt the time they were committing to the effort was being wasted. Despite my best efforts to serve as a *de facto* chief of staff to the chair, the process was not improving. The leadership challenge became critical when the chair came to me and acknowledged that we needed to do something "dramatic". I suggested that we hold a special retreat to help us get back on track, and he agreed. Engaging a number of Committee members to work as the retreat planning team, we quickly secured dates for a multi-day retreat, agreed to focus our time on leadership, and selected an experienced facilitator to help ensure our conversation would be focused and productive.

In my experience, retreats can be powerful leadership interventions when they are well planned. Upsides often include a renewed sense of purpose, deeper buy-in, and better informed and supported steps for moving forward. The approach was almost derailed when questions were raised about who would pay for the retreat, which was described to me as an "extravagant undertaking". While this was quickly resolved when it became known that the foundation had already agreed to cover the cost of the retreat, it was surprising how unusual the use of such an intervention—a multi-day retreat at a neutral location—was to the public and nonprofit partners who were struggling to work together as a committee.

Leaning on the experience gained at our initial meeting, at the retreat the group openly discussed its initial leadership process and recalled how members had set aside personal aspirations for the greater good. Given the experience of the Committee over the past six months, members were committed to ensuring that the effort had the experienced leadership it needed going forward, regardless of where this leadership came from. Many members stated that the servant leadership model used during the Committee's launch was bearing fruit and could help prevent a descent into chaos, an outcome many had expected and some were even silently hoping for as a result. The group was focused on determining who had the requisite skill set needed to advance the work, not who was most popular or most eager to lead. Committee members understood and talked openly about how the decision we were about to make could be the difference between success and failure. Members recommitted themselves to getting back on track and to ensuring the report to the Board of Supervisors was completed on time and with full participation.

The agenda also allowed time for Committee members to socialize, and included a learning component to give members opportunities to reflect and connect with one another outside of our usual meeting environment and time constraints. Given that many members had not worked together before, this proved to be essential for establishing more trusting relationships. We learned that it is imperative for leadership of equity movements to model the sharing of power from the start, and to work to intentionally help the members of multi-disciplinary groups build interpersonal as well as group trust. It is also important for differences in experience, training, perceived status, and knowledge to be openly discussed, and to allow each participant time to describe how they bring important and unique skills and value to the effort. We learned how important it is to share leadership opportunities, and did so by assigning chairs to lead committees focused on specific tasks. By the end of the retreat we had regained a good deal of our focus, agreed on an expedited timeline for finalizing the first of two reports to the county board, and redesigned our governance structure and leadership team. The group, not without debate and dissension, agreed to move from a chair and vice-chair model to one with co-equal chairs (co-chairs), who would work though a committee structure to ensure deeper engagement and alignment between committee members' skills and tasks that needed to be completed. We left the retreat with a renewed sense of urgency and a commitment from committee members to rally around the strategy and the timeline the body had adopted for moving forward.

B. Context Matters: What You Do Not Understand and/or Prepare For Can Harm You

With a renewed sense of commitment and confidence in the new leadership structure, committee members turned their full attention and energy back to developing the Committee's plan to present to the County Board of Supervisors. While the leadership team participated fully in the plan's development, we also began to focus attention on crafting a strategy for building the support required to get the plan approved. We understood that an effort that has at its center race, politics, and systemic change would naturally have critics with strong opinions about whether, who, and how the work was being conducted. Our intent was to better understand the broader context in which the work was being discussed by stakeholders who had a stake in the outcome, but at this point had little connection to the process. We hoped to advance the work not by simply crafting a plan to overwhelm our opposition, but by answering questions and getting advice in a manner we hoped would help turn non-supporters into supporters—or at least, prevent them from becoming active opponents. We believed this to be an essential part of our ability to succeed in the long term, since we would need the support of all of our partners moving forward.

To advance this strategy, the leadership team needed to have an understanding of forces—institutions, people, and issues—that could constrain progress. We initiated an environmental scan to pick up underlying concerns we knew would not be revealed in public conversations. The skeptics, as we referred to them, were concerned about a variety of things. These included a discomfort with having to find resources to fund the work, having to share decision making power with the community, having outsiders engaged in policy development, and being diverted from their preferred agenda. While these were primarily insider (public system) concerns, there were also community concerns that came to our attention as well. While these too were expressed in numerous and interesting ways, they could be summarized as an amalgamation of a profound lack of expectation and a deep sense of mistrust. The vast majority of community members I spoke with assumed this effort would never be funded, and if it was, it was likely to be at such a low level that it would not be able to make a real difference. They were also concerned that as with numerous times before, whatever resources were appropriated would likely fall into the hands of people and organizations that had little capacity or interest in authentically understanding and connecting with their community. For them, the RAACD was viewed as more of the "same old tired approach" that gets a lot of attention for a while and then disappears without ever making a difference. None of these sentiments were unique or surprising, though it was alarming to see how deeply held they were by those that offered them.

Accordingly, we began our environmental scan work by using a modified SWOT analysis to better understand the broader socio-political environment in which we were operating. For example, on the strength/opportunity side of the ledger we had a credibly studied and validated problem that rendered the question of whether there was an issue unassailable. We also had a clear and broadly expected North Star goal—a 10% to 20 % reduction in the AA child mortality rate. Third, we had an independent structure—the RAACD Committee—that was officially chartered by the County Board of Supervisors and which had a mandate to address the child mortality crisis. On the weakness/threat side of the ledger, we had concerns about the capacity of the African American community and the nonprofits in the impacted neighborhoods to take on such a complex undertaking coming from our public sector partners. We also had deep skepticism coming from community who found it hard to believe that they were going to be asked and supported to take on key roles in reducing child mortality in their neighborhoods.

I would be remiss if I failed to note that we were also aware of the broader context in which our work and these conversations were taking place. After a series of tragic events that gained national media attention, there was a growing conversation about the value of black lives in America. While no local events had come under that spotlight, the mantra and question that was being asked nationally—"Do black lives matter?"—was clearly front and center in many of the conversations we were having. I was asked more times than I can recall, "Why is this only coming to light now?" Suspicion. "Why should I believe that something is truly going to be done about a problem that has lasted for twenty years?" Skepticism. "What experience, training and capacity does the community have to be able to understand and/or respond to this problem?" Class. And, "Why is the Committee not focused on all children?" Race. I'm certain these issues—suspicion, skepticism, class, and race—are and will continue to be present in most if not all social justice and health equity, work as these, and other similar, themes are consistent contributors to existing patterns of inequality and disparity.

We were not naive and we understood that our scan would not resolve these challenges, but we believed our willingness to set aside time to engage in public and private conversations with supporters and non-supporters helped us to better understand how they would be likely to show up as we moved forward. The information gathering process was intentionally designed to be personal and engaging, as opposed to rigid and administrative. We knew we needed to connect with people in situations in which they, not us, were most comfortable. Of course, we also held community meetings, which were powerful, inspiring, and sad, all at the same time. The stories of loss and family and community struggles related to the health and well-being of children deepened our resolve to succeed. However, the private conversations, which augmented our large group discussions, were also very important. We found that individual meetings allowed conversations about delicate and often uncomfortable topics to take place; people were more likely to say what was really on their mind as opposed to what was safe. While it is hard to precisely quantify the overall impact of this process, its influence on the quality of our thinking and planning was significant.

C. Advocate – Strategic, Unapologetic, Relentless and Respectful

In March 2015, fourteen months after beginning its work, the Steering Committee submitted the first of two reports it planned to present to the County Board of Supervisors. The two-report approach, which the Committee had developed at the retreat, would include a strategic plan that would be followed by the development and submission of an implementation plan. The two-report approach allowed us to open a public dialogue about systemic transformation (strategy) without getting bogged down in debates about specific intervention (program) models. Depending on where the system change conversation landed, we would use the implementation plan to build upon the accepted systemic change concept model to design a plan for building capacity across the six most impacted communities to achieve the outcome of reduced African American child mortality rates. We believed this approach was a necessary response to concerns regarding the lack of community capacity, and the efficacy of making resources available to nascent community nonprofits.

Our approach was not to simply strike compromises; it was clear in the results of our environmental scan that our approach to engage in system change, policy, advocacy, and community engagement were all strategies we would have to strongly advocate for. The goal was to advocate thoughtfully by creating authentic opportunities for community and system leaders to engage, discuss, and create joint ownership of an issue that neither could solve alone. By doing so we hoped to foster a more open, honest, and mutually respectful relationship. This is not to suggest that we had not received thoughtful feedback during the more public aspects of our process. In fact, we had gotten a fair amount; however, the vast majority simply pointed out that we needed to be more specific about our program elements; few offered advice or direction regarding the challenge of engaging in what would be significant systemic change. Herein lies the central disconnect as our external analysis suggested that our biggest challenge was not our ability to find evidence-based or promising practices; it was the high level of skepticism, suspicion, and concern regarding our proposal to share power and decision making authority with communities, and how these ideas would be operationalized.

For example, many of the groups we identified as being best positioned to connect with youth exposed to or engaged in violence were groups so nascent by traditional standards that they would find it very difficult to meet the numerous standards required to secure public funding. We proposed connecting them to larger, more established groups by subcontract. *For many, finding a way to bring them on board was viewed as unreasonable and circumventing the vetting process.* We argued that youth engagement is essential, and that youth should be paid for the involvement. This exposure to work and making a contribution to their community were opportunities to not just start a program, but to build a healthy community. *However, for many this idea was not sufficiently connected to preventing child death.* We also argued against working in a siloed manner, engaging with only the agencies that typically come to mind when thinking about children and tragedy—child protective services or juvenile probation. We believed that a broader approach that included the hope and lift of education, opportunities to work, the recognition and healing of trauma, and early child development would be more powerful and effective. *For many this seemed too diffuse.* We also advocated from a targeted but universal position, which meant that we would target African American children, but also establish supportive child and family policy that would be good for all children. *For many, this idea seemed naive and ill-informed.* We acknowledged that the breadth of the approach was challenging, but it was in alignment with the social determinant of heath recommendation contained in the Blue Ribbon Commission report, and so we maintained our direction.

With a thoughtful and inclusive plan in hand, an analysis of the challenges we would face, and a strategy for advocating for the plan's approval, we were prepared for our presentation to the Board of Supervisors. We met with supporters and non-supporters, changed a few minds, and worked hard to mobilize community to take its necessary and rightful place in this effort through a get-out-and-participate campaign organized and carried out by grass roots advocates, faith leaders, and young adults. On a warm afternoon in mid-May 2015, as the County Board of Supervisors convened to discuss the county's health and human service budget, over one hundred and fifty community supporters showed up to offer their support for the Committee's plan to reduce African American child mortality. They were joined in solidarity by about fifty other advocates, who were there to support healthcare for undocumented children. Clad in yellow Black Children's Lives Matter t-shirts, with All Children's Lives Matter emblazoned on the back, several attendees chose to advocate for both causes; even members from organized labor, there for other reasons, stepped to the microphone to urge support for our cause. My co-chair, Wendy Petko, and I presented the plan to the board, which requested an annual commitment of US$2.25 million over five years to build community capacity to reduce disproportionate African American child mortality rates in six communities, by establishing a grass roots public education campaign using authentic community influencers, strengthening neighborhood nonprofit operating capacity, increasing community participation in child and family policy discussions, launching a participatory action research program to track progress, and establishing an Interagency Children's Policy Council to review and respond to challenges and opportunities to improve the health status and well-being of all children. The Board approved the proposed plan, moved the financing decision to the final budget hearing and requested the non-budget item, planning for the establishment of an ICPC, to begin immediately.

At the final budget hearing in mid-June 2015 the Committee presented its plan to operationalize its strategic plan by connecting six community lead institutions together to form a network capable of achieving the scale required to reduce the county's African American child mortality rate by 10% to 20% over a five-year period. The updated approach added specificity by including a description of a faculty-based Technical Assistance and Resource Center to strengthen neighborhood nonprofits' operating capacity, the inclusion of youth voices in the development of a grass youth communications, public education, and social media campaign, and the selection of Community Incubator Leads (community-based nonprofits who would serve as launch points for programs and contracting entities to engage and support non-traditional service providers). The implementation plan built upon the strategic plan's initial recommendations that were focused on leveraging influencers and establishing a resident leadership council to support and inform RAACD Committee deliberations. The presentation was attended by approximately one hundred and twenty-five community members who once again voiced their support for the plan. Without dissent, the County board approved a five-year, US$7.5 million funding commitment to support the effort as presented.

V. Conclusion

It might be impossible for me to write a thoughtful conclusion about an effort that in many ways is merely at its beginning. Admittedly, the process involved in getting to this point could be described as a journey in itself, but I have no false illusions about the fact that the most challenging, but potentially the most rewarding, part of our journey is about to begin. Accordingly, I want to thank the incredible number of individuals who have offered words of support during difficult periods to the Committee and to me personally. Our success is borne of their belief and hope that a better future for African American children in Sacramento will be achieved. To my former co-chair Wendy Petko, thanks for your calm and powerful leadership. And to the full Committee, you are to be commended for keeping the real reason we were convened front and center during difficult times. Finally, there is evidence that our approach is working. Several months ago two Committee members, Dr. Ethan Cutts, and Diane Galati, who represent large hospital systems, announced that their institution had begun conducting sleep assessment with the parents of all children, regardless of race, who are born in their hospitals. Each new parent would be educated on how a baby should be positioned to sleep, and if they did not have a safe sleeping environment they would be given one at no cost. This effort will reach approximately 70% of all new parents in the Sacramento region. Equity can benefit us all.

"*A luta continua*" (let the struggle continue).

References

Blue Ribbon Commission Report. 2015. *African American Children Matter: What we Must Do Now*. Sacramento, CA: County of Sacramento http://www. shfcenter.org/assets/Steering%20Committee/RAACD_Strategic_Plan_Report_ March_2015.pdf. Accessed May 2, 2016.

Braveman, P. & S. Gruskin. 2003. Defining equity in health. *Journal of Epidemiol Community Health*. 57: 254-258 doi:10.1136/jech.57.4.254

Kania, J. & M. Kramer. 2011. Collective impact. *Stanford Social Innovation Review*. Winter. http://ssir.org/articles/entry/collective_impact. Accessed April 29, 2016.

8   Social Impact Bonds

Legal and Leadership Considerations

Dru Bhattacharya, JD, MPH, LLM

I. Introduction

Social Impact Bonds (SIBs) are contracts that have been suggested as a cost-beneficial alternative to public-private partnerships to support social services. The arrangements involve lenders who invest a significant amount of upfront capital in preventive interventions whose established effectiveness mitigates the risk of financial loss. They have been implemented worldwide with success, but they are novel constructs within the context of public health interventions. Against a backdrop of fiscal constraints, the investment of significant capital to generate significant cost-savings with the risk disproportionately held by lenders—with the possibility of significant returns on investment as a cut in response to those savings—is a potentially quite lucrative venture. Additionally, this involves a transfer of risk from the taxpayer, to whom the government is not liable for any ineffective or inefficient rendering of services, to a third party lender who disproportionately bears the financial risk.

SIBs are recent interventions that began in the United Kingdom and have recently made their way to the United States. The first SIB was launched in the U.K. in 2010. That program was specifically designed to reduce recidivism at Peterborough prison by supporting the reintegration of prisoners into the community. Initial evaluation was promising with the rate of recidivism among newly released prisoners at 8.4%, exceeding minimum thresholds of success (7.5%). In the U.S., New York City launched the first SIB that was also focused on reducing recidivism, but this time among 3,000 youths who had been incarcerated at Riker's Island. In 2013 Fresno became the site of a demonstration project on home-based intervention on whose results, if successful, would lead to a program expansion funded by a SIB.

Against this backdrop, a legal and leadership assessment of social impact bonds is a timely contribution for health departments who do not have a significant body of literature to assess the typical challenges they would face in implementing such agreements. The typical rights, duties, and liabilities of interested parties are legitimate inquiries that ought to be clearly articulated by any governmental agencies considering an adoption of these instruments to advance the delivery of services to secure population health. However, a more thorough review of some of these agreements indicates a more complicated legal landscape in practice. Moreover, the ever-changing political and public health context, within which these agreements must necessarily operate, heavily influences their structure, thereby creating unique provisions within each contract (particularly as relates to evaluation and payment).

The objectives of this chapter are four-fold; we shall review the general structure of social impact bonds that have been executed. The structure is more or less consistent with the predictable boilerplate language, but there are some particular elements of these contracts that ought to be highlighted. Next, we provide some specific examples from city and state contracts against a backdrop of current events and developments. This is where the potential differences in terms and interpretation may become amplified. We shall then summarize some trends and provide some general recommendations to facilitate deliberations among stakeholders who may wish to adopt these measures. Finally, we re-examine these general recommendations in the context of leadership considerations for public health departments.

II. General Structure of a SIB and the agreement

The general structure of a SIB involves a lender or investor who provides an investment to an intermediary between the lender and the government. The intermediary directs the working capital to the service provider, who provides data and information to an independent evaluator to validate program outcomes. Upon validation, the government will then direct performance payment, i.e. with principal and interest, to the lender. These relationships are captured in the figure below.

The general structure of these agreements is also fairly predictable insofar as they mirror a typical contract. We find provisions covering:

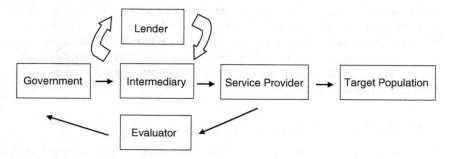

Figure 8.1 General Structure of a SIB

(1) an introduction of the terms and purpose, (2) performance targets, (3) payments and third party fees, (4) oversight and reporting, (5) representations, warranties, and covenants, and (6) remedies. At the outset, let us draw our attention to performance targets, as well as oversights and reporting, which together would constitute the basis for foreseeable developments in potentially modifying the contract, breaches, or early termination.

A. Performance Targets

Beyond those explicit terms that speak to the mutual assent of the parties, an enforceable contract requires that the terms be definite and certain. Here is where clarity in performance targets among the parties is critical. A formal Evaluation Plan is incorporated and ought to include the specific criteria for evaluating performance, as well as the methodology employed.

When we examine these provisions from a public health perspective, we cannot stress enough how critical it is for parties to be transparent about the strength of methods used to assess achievement. For example, epidemiological studies include observational and experimental studies, which have different levels of strength that consequently restrain the inferences that we may draw from the analyses. Depending on the evaluation, we may or may not be able to assess the effectiveness, or more accurately, the precise association between a program and the observed outcomes.

Surveys are often conducted because they are relatively cheap and provide immediate information about a population of interest. However, their inherent limitation is in that snapshot, which measures all responses at a single point in time. While this may allow us to examine the correlation between some characteristics (e.g. if there is a relationship between, say, coffee consumption and cancer), we cannot tease out which factor preceded the other. So if we noted a strong correlation between the two, we could not determine if it was the consumption of coffee that increased the odds of subsequent incidence of cancer, or whether those individuals in our sample simply consumed more coffee as a lifestyle choice. This constraint in surveys and related cross-sectional studies in epidemiology illustrate the principle that causation implies correlation, but the corollary does not necessarily hold true. Determinations of causality require further (and costlier) studies that examine the relationship among factors over time to overcome this hurdle.

B. Oversight and Reporting

A Steering Committee, composed of local or national experts, may raise concerns, discuss trends, or simply monitor progress. They may be called upon to hold meetings and issue reports based on their deliberations and findings. It is important here to discuss if and how many representatives a lender may be entitled to place on the Committee; to maintain objectivity and avoid any conflicts of interest, these representatives will likely not have a right to vote on any matter before the Committee. These Committees often retain the power to call for special meetings to address urgent matters within a reasonable timeframe, usually two or three business days.

Even if an intervention is established, unforeseen events or other considerations may require a change in implementation. The Committee should be made up of a diverse body of experts and representatives who may deliberate on issues when faced with the challenge of securing the interests, at times conflicting, of both the lender and the government.

III. Example One: City of Chicago and Child Parent Center Social Impact Bond

The first example we shall examine is an agreement executed in fall 2014 between the City of Chicago and IFF Pay for Success, LLC, known as the Child Parent Center (CPC) Social Impact Bond. The purpose of this program was to promote readiness for kindergarten in language and literacy, engage parents, and enhance educational attainment.

Based on the general structure discussed above, the Child Parent Center SIB may be depicted as seen in Figure 8.2.

The contract was executed between the City of Chicago (government) through its Department of Family and Support Services and IFF Pay for Success I, LLC (the lender) with payments directed to and through the Board of Education of the City of Chicago to the Child Parent Centers operated by the Board. IFF is an Illinois non-profit corporation and is the sole member of IFF Pay for Success I, LLC. The contract was formally executed between the city and the lender, and followed the establishment of an ordinance transmitted on October 8, 2014, by the Mayor, Rahm Emanuel, together with Aldermen Moreno, Ervin, Balcer, Suarez, and Mitts, authorizing an issuance of SIBs.

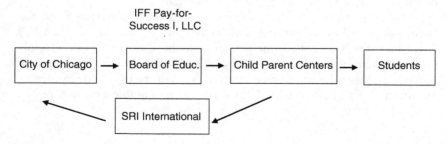

Figure 8.2 City of Chicago SIB

The program had three primary impact outcomes, including: (1) Special Educational Utilization, (2) Kindergarten Readiness, and (3) Third Grade Literacy. The questions that guide their assessments are:

1   What is the impact of the program on the rate at which they need an Individualized Education Plan, or IEP?
2   What is the impact on Kindergarten Readiness on Teaching Strategies or TS Gold?
3   What is the impact on third grade literacy as defined by performance on CPS third grade assessment?

Impacts are estimated using the total population of eligible students at the sites, and then scaled to reflect the number of seats funded by the lenders, and of course adjusted for any mobility trends.

A. Defining Primary Impact Outcomes: Standards Ought to be Specified based on (Un)certainty of Performance

At first glance, the assessments are seemingly straightforward. For the Special Education Utilization, the primary outcome is a binary indicator of whether or not a student has a CPS-issued Individualized Education Plan or IEP in a given year. This is a data point provided as part of the regular data collection points by CPS. If the student has a diagnosis on his or her IEP of a severe disability, that student is removed from the study pool; this is collected annually from K to sixth grade. For Kindergarten Readiness, we find use of the Teaching Strategies or TS Gold instrument to track the development of children in pre-K classrooms. This measures their progress in socio-emotional, physical, language, literacy, and cognitive development. This is a national standard used in Head Start programs with the primary outcome metric being the share of kids who are performing at or above the national trends across five of six domains, including: (1) literacy, (2) language, (3) math, (4) cognitive development, (5) socio-emotional, (6) and physical health. It is when we come to the third grade literacy that we begin to appreciate that the standard we use ought to be based on the certainty of performance.

At the time of drafting the agreement and the Evaluation Plan, the Partnership for Assessment of Readiness for College and Careers (PAARC) exam had not been rolled out yet, though the Chicago Public Schools were anticipating that they would do so. Therefore, they included language that noted this and some discretion on the part of the evaluator to suggest an alternative test or metric. Afterwards, some notable and unforeseen developments unfolded.

B. *Ensuring Contract has Specificity to Weather Political and Performance Setbacks*

In January 2015, CPS decided to only administer the exam to 10% of eligible schools, citing technology as a factor. Officials at the Illinois State Board of Education were not amused and threatened sanctions, including immediate loss of funding. In March 2015 CPS announced that it would expand PAARC to all eligible schools, and some officials publicly noted the financial sanctions as the major reason why they decided to comply, notwithstanding their initial position.

In this case the agreement actually anticipated the possibility of modifications for this third outcome, and explicitly stated: "Any modifications must be made prior to the first cohort starting Third Grade, and must be approved by CPS, the City, the Project Coordinator, and approved by the Lender Committee." Another issue is the effect of opt-outs on the part of parents; unless we see a significant number doing so, this probably won't be an issue, but if it were a problem this clause might arguably cover any modifications responding to those developments, although the language does state that they must be made prior to the first cohort starting third grade.

Since we are dealing with contracts and outcomes in the potential midst of political and performance setbacks, there are a couple notable features that ought to be considered. First, stakeholders ought to be flexible in assessing a primary outcome. Here, the parties anticipated adapting the methodology in response to how it was being implemented. Specifically, "the exact methodology for calculating Third Grade Literacy may have to be adapted pending observation of how the test is being administered, scored, etc.", and "[i]n the event that fewer than 50% of students are scoring above the 25th percentile, the Evaluator will propose a new protocol or test for determining [literacy] that better captures the performance of students." This flexibility illustrates how assessment is an iterative process.

Stakeholders should also consider including a draft protocol to potentially recalculate payments. Here, they included draft language to recalculate payments based on a fixed rate and share of students satisfying a threshold outcome. Specifically, the number of treatment group students who read at or above grade level would be multiplied by "the base cohort size, multiplied by cumulative mobility from the Third Grade year of a given cohort", which would then be multiplied by the fixed payment rate of $750 to determinate the total payments owed by the City for that cohort.

C. *Investigating Highly Unexpected Outcomes*

There is always a chance that outcomes may be unexpected, perhaps even surprising. In this agreement, the parties anticipated some precise scenarios that would enable the Evaluator to validate the findings. Among them were situations where there were negative or no statistically different associations in rates for any cohort in any year after Kindergarten. In effect, the program was not making things any better, or perhaps was making things worse. Another possibility was that the "No Pre-K" group had a utilization rate that was 2.5 times higher than the treatment group. A third situation involved highly irregular patterns where utilization might be down by over 2% or up by over 7%. In the event of any of these scenarios, the Evaluator has complete discretion to validate the findings. To be clear, these situations do not necessarily relieve a party of accountability or liability, but simply ensure that the results were not an error in assessment.

Chicago's program also had five qualitative research questions that were meant to improve program performance, including:

1   How do outcomes vary by subgroups (e.g. sex, race, English language learner status)?
2   How is the program impacting attendance in Pre-K?
3   How does the program support the transition to K?
4   How successful is the program at improving social-emotional learning outcomes?
5   How successful is the program at engaging parents?

Notably, these inquiries were unrelated to the payment calculations. They did, however, speak to trends and issues that would be of importance to our understanding of how the program affects different subgroups along the lines of race, sex, and language, as well as the levels of parental engagement, all of which may affect the outcomes. The overarching objective is to improve program performance unrelated to the Pay for Success calculations.

Anticipated return on investments will vary, so articulating the anticipated payment along with caps is critical for clarity in the pay schedule. For the City of Chicago contract, anticipated payments from "savings" and "success" payments for greater-than-expected results indicated a high return on investment (see Table 8.1).

Additionally, some contracts might include additional payments for highly successful results. Here, the anticipated payments were a little

Table 8.1 City of Chicago SIB Loan, Payments, and Escrowed Funds

Initial loan(s)	$16,651,292
Anticipated payments	$21,481,790
Maximum payments	$30,000,000
Escrowed 'pay-for-success' funds	$4,369,770

over $21 million, but the ceiling was set at $30 million. If the program yields a much higher level of success than anticipated, the lenders could obtain an additional $4.5 million dollars. This particular agreement is potentially quite lucrative, with an initial investment of $16.5 million and the potential to recoup over twice that amount over the course of the program.

IV. Example Two: Massachusetts Social Innovation Financing Youth Recidivism Initiative

In Massachusetts the state executed an agreement for the Social Innovation Financing Youth Recidivism Initiative between the Commonwealth of Massachusetts, Roca, Inc., and Youth Services, Inc. The objective was to help youth move out of violence and poverty with outcomes related to reductions in incarceration and improved job readiness and employment, using a cognitive-behavioral intervention model known as the Roca Intervention Model. The outcomes were related to reductions in incarceration, improved job readiness, and employment. Eligibility criteria included being male, aged 17 to 21, residing in a pre-specified town or city, and having signed a consent and release form to be referred to services and have their outcomes followed.

A striking feature of this agreement is the sheer rigor of its evaluation plan. It proposes a randomized control trial (RCT) which is the gold standard of measuring the effectiveness of the program on achieving improve outcomes. Earlier, we identified different kinds of studies with varying levels of strengths and limitations that may restrain our ability to gauge effectiveness. The RCT is at the top of that pyramid and is able to longitudinally assess the relationship among factors over a period of time, thereby providing evidence of causality. Now, a technical caveat in implementation is obtaining a higher fraction of treatment group participants who end up enrolling in the program. That aside, this is one way, albeit a costly one, to establish rigor. It also offers the highest probability or certainty of establishing a correlation between the program and the observed outcomes. Employment outcomes included the total number of eligible quarters in which an individual is employed. Recidivism outcomes were "bed days" avoided, while educational outcomes—with no basis for payment—reflected high school graduation and GED completion.

As in the Chicago example, Massachusetts had flexibility in its evaluation methodology, with a backstop methodology in anticipation of a potentially lower fraction of individuals in its treatment group enrolling in the program. The provision articulated an action plan in anticipation of a potentially lower fraction ($< .30$) of individuals in the treatment group who enrolled in the program.

The employment outcomes were also clearly indicated and included a 40% reduction of bed-days of incarceration, which corresponded to

199,293 bed-days; and a 30% increase in employment quarters, or approximately 1,113 employment quarters. There is interest on these loans, with the Senior Loan bearing 5% per annum and the Junior Loan bearing 2%. This heightened level of evaluation with the RCT, together with the precision of loan terms, demonstrates meticulous planning to secure the optimal return on investment.

V. Example Three: Counter-Argument against Reentry Programming in Maryland

In 2013, the Department of Legislative Services in Maryland issued a case study of its own social impact bond that offered some constructive criticism of these arrangements. This 2013 case study on the Reentry Programming in Maryland offers a set of counter-arguments against the use of SIBs. Among the central arguments included: (1) the broader need for an investment market with a higher degree of risk tolerance, (2) the need for enforcement measures to prevent early termination, citing Massachusetts' termination clause on the part of lenders within two years if the program isn't performing up to expectations, (3) the fact that the high stakes payments may distort evidence, and (4) the fact that a single evaluation may be inconclusive.

These points are well taken, but I would like to offer some considerations in response to the early termination rights and evaluation methods. Both the state and the lender had rights of early termination in Massachusetts, but as we shall see, the conditions differ in terms of what triggers the exercise of that right. Moreover, in Massachusetts we had the gold standard of evaluation in the randomized control trial. However, this costly course of action is not always feasible, not to mention having to be budgeted in advance. So it is not so much how many evaluations that are conducted, but the type of evaluation, along with the budget constraints, that ought to guide our assessments of their effectiveness.

Rights to terminate participation or discontinue funding are critical components of the contract. In Massachusetts, the Commonwealth's early termination right provided, in the relevant part: "If on the last day of Quarter 8 or Quarter 12, the cumulative Attrition Rate of Roca Youth exceeds 350% of the applicable cumulative Historic Attrition Rate, the Commonwealth, by notice given to the Parties with copies to the Lenders and the Grantors within ten days after the end of Quarter 8 or Quarter 12 (as applicable), may terminate Roca's participation under this Contract." On the part of the Lender, "If on the last day of Project Quarter 8, (A) the Attrition Rate of Roca Youth exceeds 250%, but is less than 350%, of the applicable historic attrition rate (the "Historic Attrition Rate") and (B) either (x) Senior Lender has funded an amount equal to $3,300,000 or (y) the number of Roca Youth is at least 650 and Senior Lender has funded its *pro rata* share of the Project Fees to allow for the full Roca

Intervention Model to be provided to all Roca Youth enrolled as of the last day of Project Quarter 8, Senior Lender will have the right to discontinue funding of the Senior Loan." Thus the State has a threshold of attrition, and the Lender has a lower threshold, but must also satisfy an additional monetary investment or enrollment of participants. However, the parties retain the discretion to determine whether these rights and conditions are proportionate to the risks that each party has undertaken.

In Massachusetts, the program can be modified without terminating it if things take a turn for the worse. The contract provides for a Corrective Action Plan with action triggers. The provision provides that: "If on the last day of Project Quarter 8, the Attrition Rate of Roca Youth exceeds 200% and Senior Lender does not exercise its Early Termination Right, the Lenders, Borrower and Roca will agree to a plan of decreased enrollment of Roca Youth for subsequent Project Quarters and a corresponding modification of the Funding Schedule in order to reduce costs of the Project and to allow for the full Roca Intervention Model to be provided to all Roca Youth enrolled as of the end of Project Quarter 12." In other words, if the attrition rate hit a threshold of 200%, and the lender did not exercise its Early Termination Right, it would agree to a modified plan with a different funding schedule to lower costs. While this suggests a degree of flexibility, the dispositive issue for those considering these arrangements concerns if and when the lender ought to be given the right to terminate or modify the plan.

In summary, the legal challenges are highly case-specific. In Maryland, we saw high operational costs with the design of the contract estimated at $300,000 and a net fiscal impact of over $3 million in variable and fixed costs, including the program evaluation, direct services, and management fee. In Massachusetts, we saw rigorous evaluation models but also termination clauses based on complex performance indicators and enrollment thresholds. In Chicago, compliance for one of three primary outcomes was based on an unproven performance metric against a volatile political backdrop.

We may therefore glean some general recommendations from this cursory review, and parties should: (1) define terms that are definite and certain, to the extent possible, (2) incorporate backup methodologies for evaluation, (3) specify rights and conditions of termination for the government and lenders, and (4) articulate caps on payments based on savings and success.

VI. Leadership Considerations for Public Health Departments

To this point, we have focused on the structure of SIBs and the attendant rights and duties of parties to the contract. Here we reexamine these issues in the context of leadership considerations for health departments. On March 25, 2013 Social Finance, Inc. and Collective Health announced an award of $660,000 in grant funding to launch a demonstration project, collect data, and evaluate the results. This project would lay the groundwork for the first health-related SIB in the U.S. With over 20% of children diagnosed with asthma in the affected area, the prevalence and healthcare costs were estimated at $35 million annually. The SIB program engaged over two hundred low-income children with asthma to provide home care, education, and support to decrease environmental determinants.

By December 2015 the intervention phase of the project was complete, to be followed by an evaluation of Medi-Cal claims data to analyze the effect of the in-home asthma intervention programs as relates to program outcomes and costs. While anecdotal evidence suggests improvements— with some parents reporting up to 80% fewer emergency department visits and 70% reductions in asthma-related hospitalizations—the final report will likely determine the opportunity to scale up the model and its reach via an SIB.

From a leadership perspective, program management and evaluation is subsequent to program planning, and notwithstanding the results of one project this raises a number of issues that ought to be considered for long-term planning, particularly as it relates to the roles and responsibilities of health departments. The Fresno demonstration project stemmed from a proposal by two non-profit organizations (Social Finance, Inc. and Collective Health), and was justified by disturbing trends in childhood asthma. In 2014 the American Lung Association declared that Fresno was suffering the worst exposure to air pollution, coupled with the highest rates of asthma nationwide, creating a perfect storm that would make an environmental health-related intervention among the top (if not the top) priority of public health interventions. It is indeed difficult to envision a community where 20% of children diagnosed with asthma might be reluctant to welcome the influx of working capital to alleviate this burden.

In practice, however, not every city or target population will experience the kind of extreme characterizations that would likely receive majority (if not unanimous) support from stakeholders. A notable feature of the general model of SIBs is that the target audience—the downstream population—is something of an offshoot of the stakeholders. Consequently, the planning of these arrangements is, by and large, a product of communication between two groups of stakeholders, namely the parties to the contract. What is problematic in this arrangement is that the intervention is driven by a choice of services that will likely be heavily weighted by the projected return on investment.

Here, I propose the development of an arrangement that is, at the very least, informed by the input of the affected population in what I dub 'Community-Based Participatory Investment' (CBPI), modeled after the effectiveness of community-based participatory research (CBPR). CBPR is unique in that it involves neighborhood organizations, community residents, and other community stakeholders to recruit subjects, acquire firsthand knowledge of the experience of health problems, and later become champions of interventions based on the research findings. Two central themes of CBPR are community empowerment and social justice, providing members with a sense of ownership over the process and reducing the traditional power imbalance between researchers and residents by democratizing the research. In a similar vein, a CBPI model would result in arrangements that are informed by community representatives in the development and planning phase of the SBI. While critics may point to the presence of community representatives on steering committees, these bodies are created after the fact, and while members certainly have a vote their voices are a response to concerns or trends after the intervention has already been implemented. What is required is an upstream presence that participates in deliberations between the government and the lender prior to the execution of the agreement. This model would alter the general model discussed earlier by inserting community representatives into the scheme, as depicted in Figure 8.3.

With respect to public health departments and their leadership, engaging community representatives ought to be part of a broader strategic plan as relates to the organization. This may be challenging if the department does not have a strategic plan at the level of intervention, thereby delegating the determination of need and benefit squarely within the domain of decision-makers far removed from the affected populations.

The general purpose of strategic planning is to streamline organizational decisions based on an overarching mission, values, goals, and objectives. In contrast with operational planning, its focus is on external considerations. In doing this, planning is an essential leadership function that bridges the policy, administrative, and public health domains.

As a preliminary matter, the health department should consider the following questions:

1 Does the department have a strategic plan? If so, is it updated to address the pressing unmet needs of its constituents? If not, consider engaging a partner to collaborate in developing one.
2 Does the proposed SBI align with the vision, mission, and values of the department as articulated in its strategic plan?

Given the potential breadth of stakeholders, including public and private entities, a strategic plan should also be developed specifically for the fund. Input ought to be acquired from community residents, the fund's advisory board, and others with a vested interest in the fund's programs and activities. The fund's strategic plan should also be consistent with the strategic plan of the public health department(s) charged with securing the health of the affected populations at the local, county, or state levels.

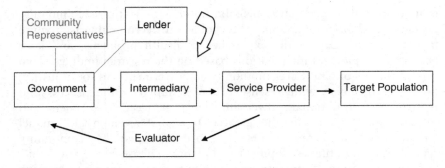

Figure 8.3 Revised Structure of an SIB based on a CBPI model

In the absence of such plans, public health officials ought to be approached for participation in, or to provide feedback to, the fund's development of its strategic plan.

Critical issues may be avoided by anticipating where conflicts may arise in the alignment of goals and objectives, action steps, and evaluative criteria. Articulating these issues allows for a more robust deliberation by all stakeholders, including many who may be unaware of the breadth of public health issues that a community may be facing. It also provides an objective standard of metrics that are removed from any profit motive and based solely on addressing the unmet health needs of the population. There are also numerous assessment tools that extend beyond a mere cost-benefit analysis that may be employed to assess the program's strengths and weakness, thereby creating opportunities for improvement.

In their present form, SIBs present health departments with an opportunity to engage in two core functions of public health, namely assurance and assessment, by linking services to affected population and evaluating the effects of those interventions. We may add policy development to this list by mobilizing community partnerships by requesting input in the planning stages and representation on steering committees charged with oversight and monitoring of the program's progress.

While assurance, assessments, and policy development are distinct, they are also mutually reinforcing so that an alignment of all three enables moments of ethical clarity whereby leaders may institute change. Leaders are uniquely positioned to engage in values clarification, and among them is the courage to advocate on behalf of the most vulnerable populations. Advocacy can take many forms, and though the direction of services to these populations is a laudable enterprise, the sheer size of working capital that is often made available ought to give us pause against a backdrop of fundamental causes of disturbing trends in health disparities. Over eight years ago, Ezzati found that between 1983 and 1999 men's life expectancy in the U.S. decreased in over fifty counties nationwide, and for women there was an even more shocking result in that their life expectancy decreased in more than nine hundred counties. Although these statistics are disturbing in and of themselves, the common thread that pervades most health disparities is the concentration of poor health among the disadvantaged. Poor individuals tend to get sicker and die sooner compared to their rich counterparts, and although SIBs invariably direct resources to improve the conditions of disadvantaged populations, they do not address the fundamental causes of health disparities.

Now it behooves us to note that the purpose of SIBs is not to alleviate poverty, but to ensure the availability of funds to render services to and presumably *for* the poor. This presents a paradox for public health leaders. The necessity of short-term gains countervails the patience required to align disadvantaged populations with resources—education being chief among them—to serve as protective factors and move our discourse beyond traditional risk factor identification and downstream intervention. Perhaps a portion of the funds based on the initial investment or estimated cost savings could be directed towards those upstream determinants based on a social epidemiological profile of the target population. Unfortunately, the characterization of determinants and the distribution of illness are often restricted to proximal factors related to the clinical manifestation of illness or its management and treatment, rather than its root causes. So as public health officials contemplate how best to leverage the influx of working capital to alleviate the burden of illness among disadvantaged populations, a preliminary step would be the incorporation of a social epidemiological profile into reports that are utilized to suggest the merits of a SIB. In doing this, all stakeholders will have a nuanced appreciation of the myriad of factors contributing to the current trends and, more importantly, the unmet needs of the population.

VII. Lessons from the Adolescent Behavioral Learning Program at Riker's Island

In August 2015 the independent evaluator of the Adolescent Behavioral Learning Experience Program at Riker's Island reported its findings on whether the program had reduced recidivism among young people aged 16 to 18 who were detained at Riker's Island prison in New York City. It assessed recidivism bed-days to capture the number of days individuals were detained in the prison during the twelve months following their release. A quasi-experimental design was implemented in lieu of an RCT for practical purposes (adolescents were said to frequently move between units, thereby confounding the treatment and control groups). The Vera group's evaluation indicated that the program did not reduce recidivism for participants and, adjusted for external factors, the difference was not statistically significant when compared to the comparison group.

At first glance, critics may characterize the Riker's program a failure and be reluctant to support SIBs in the future. This reflexive response would be understandable given the attempt to extrapolate findings of studies on a smaller scale and simply expect a correlation of equal magnitude in results once the program is scaled up. In practice, however, the effect of variables, individually and in their *interaction* with one another, is complex and does not always follow a predictable pathway, notwithstanding the lengths to which data analysts may go to create a mathematical algorithm. This program is a reminder that SIBs are ultimately an investment in people, and such arrangements should be structured with stakeholders mindful of the unpredictability of human behavior and with past performance being no guarantee of future success. When parties reduce people to performance measures in a discipline that is highly contextual, and far removed from the exactness of a pure science, there are bound to be programs that disappoint. This reiterates how a deliberate effort to engage in robust strategic planning at the governmental and program levels may mitigate the factors that may compromise results, and enable adjustments in real time that ensure some positive outcomes.

VIII. Conclusion

The general structure and allocation of risk make SIBs an appealing alternative to unrealized government investments using taxpayer dollars. If the return on investment was absolute, the lender would be nothing more than a catalyst to accelerate what the government would have already done to save its limited budget. If the return was far less certain, the lender would be akin to a researcher trying to develop an evidence base and remaining hopeful that the results of this particular experiment will yield beneficial outcomes for the treatment group.

Here, we have offered a more nuanced treatment of the legal and leadership issues that invariably arise, if not in the planning phases of the arrangement, then certainly in its actual implementation. A review of two SIBs in Massachusetts and Illinois illustrate the need for precise terminology in the contractual language, the specification of rights and conditions of termination on the part of all parties, the enumeration of evaluative measures (and particularly contingency plans), and an explicit cap on payments based on savings and success.

Leadership considerations are neither initiated by the execution of the contract nor completed upon its implementation. The active engagement in assessment, assurance, and policy development ought to inform the alignment of the SIB with existent strategic plans and utilize the input of community stakeholders before formalizing the precise rights, duties, and remuneration for future services.

The dearth of health-related SIBs, together with the unflattering results of the Riker's program, only heighten anticipation of the results from the asthma management project in Fresno, and how investors will respond to those findings. It is critical to note, however, that we must be as wary of success as we are of failure in these instances. The unique populations and determinants demonstrate how the success of each SIB is highly case-specific, and results must be interpreted within the narrow context of the intervention and its target population. Health departments are uniquely situated to weigh in on the selection of interventions, articulate the kinds of data that ought to be collected, and participate in the kind of project management and oversight that ensure that the health of the public is the paramount consideration throughout the course of the project. As governmental budgets become further constrained, engaging novel public-private partnerships will become necessary for agency officials. SIBs may not be a panacea for social ills, but they do provide an opportunity that ought to be further explored with cautious optimism, and tempered with the humility that comes with transparent and representative deliberations.

9 Improving Population Health through Clinical–Community Collaboration

A Case Study of a Collaboration between State Government and an Academic Health System

Kenneth W. Kizer, MD, MPH

I. Introduction

The health of a society's population is foundational to its stability, creativity, and productivity. Thus, findings in recent years that American population health lags behind that of other developed countries has been a cause for concern (Institute of Medicine 2013; Squires and Anderson 2015), and especially so when considering that the United States spends far more on healthcare than other developed countries.

Foundational to the paradox of greater healthcare spending but poorer health outcomes are two realities that are just beginning to be broadly recognized and addressed in the U.S. The first of these is that the medical care system is significantly limited in its ability to achieve better health and that nonmedical social factors—e.g. education, employment, housing, transportation, food security, and lifestyle—materially influence health and are more important to improving population health than healthcare per se. The second reality is that the traditional American market-based fee-for-service method of paying for healthcare services has resulted in healthcare providers emphasizing the volume of services over their value, and this has driven the provision of ever more services without sufficient attention being paid to whether the services are truly needed or are yielding a good return on investment in terms of health outcomes—i.e. whether they are providing good health value. In recognition of these realities, current healthcare reform efforts seek to increasingly pay for healthcare services via various value-based payment methodologies, which inherently embody require-ments that healthcare providers focus on the social determinants of health (Burwell 2015; Health Care Transformation Task Force 2015), as well as providing appropriate, safe, and effective medical care.

Addressing the social determinants of health requires collaboration between clinical care providers and the communities they serve (i.e. "clinical-community collaborations"), although few successful and sustainable models for such collaborations currently exist. This chapter describes a seemingly successful collaboration between an operating unit within an academic health center (the Institute for Population Health Improvement in the University of California Davis Health System) and the California state government. This partnership, or collaboration, seeks to improve population health within California's highly diverse population by assisting various health-related agencies within California state government address the many determinants of health. As healthcare payment reform progresses, the need for these types of clinical-community collaborations will grow.

II. Background and Context

Achieving and maintaining good population health requires that the many determinants of health be aligned to promote and sustain good health. As such, population health is inherently a broad societal matter that transcends healthcare per se. However, population health improvement is an integral part of the *'triple aim'* that is central to current efforts to reform American healthcare and the new value-based healthcare payment models associated with these reform efforts (Berwick et al. 2008; Whittington et al. 2015). Originally proposed by Don Berwick MD and his colleagues at the Boston-based Institute for Health Improvement in 2005, the triple aim seeks to promote new models of care, which will simultaneously improve the patient experience of care (including quality and satisfaction), improve the health of populations, and reduce the per capita cost of healthcare. Subsequently, when Dr. Berwick became the Administrator of the federal Centers for Medicare and Medicaid Services, the triple aim became a core tenet of national healthcare reform strategies and central to state-based and private sector healthcare reform efforts. Multiple models of value-based payment are currently being tested, including various forms of pay for performance, episode of care bundled payment, accountable care organizations, and patient-centered medical homes. Strategies aimed at improving population health are inherent to all these payment models.

Typical of an emerging discipline, population health and population health management have been variously defined, and there is no universally agreed definition of these terms at present. In my work over the past decade or so I have defined **population health** as *the overall health status or health outcomes of a specified group of people resulting from the many determinants of health, including healthcare, public health interventions, and social and environmental factors.* Similarly, I have defined **population health management** as *taking purposeful actions to influence the health status or health outcomes of a specified group of people through coordination, integration and alignment of healthcare, public health interventions, and social and environmental determinants of health.*

Populations may be specified or defined by, among other characteristics: demographic factors such as age, sex, occupation, race, geography, or military service status; environmental factors such as exposure to air pollution, heat or cold, industrial chemicals, pesticides, or ionizing radiation; or clinical conditions such as cancer, diabetes, hypertension, hyperlipidemia, or trauma.

The underlying philosophies, principles, practices, and subject matter content of population health and public health substantially overlap. Some academicians consider them to be essentially the same. Nonetheless, there are significant differences in how they have been operationalized.

In modern history public health has been primarily a government activity, albeit with significant footprints in academia, philanthropy, and industry. Public health practice has focused primarily on effecting population-level disease prevention and health promotion interventions that have been authorized by law or policy to be conducted *within governmental jurisdictions* (e.g. nations, states, or counties). Typical public health functions include monitoring communicable diseases and investigating epidemics, ensuring safe food and potable water, remediating environmental hazards, tracking certain non-communicable diseases, and encouraging healthy behaviors. The scope and nature of public health interventions may materially differ in neighboring governmental jurisdictions and at different levels of government. Some public health agencies in recent years have actively engaged in addressing social determinants of health such as housing and employment, but this is not the norm.

Population health includes traditional public health functions and similarly seeks to reduce health disparities and improve overall health, but places a greater emphasis on coordinating or linking population-level disease prevention and health promotion activities with individual healthcare. Indeed, the triple aim of healthcare reform and the new value-based healthcare payment models being implemented to actualize the triple aim are increasingly forcing healthcare providers to think more holistically about the health of their patients and to consider the delivery of healthcare services within the broader context of the many determinants of health, including education and health literacy, employment, housing, food security, and transportation. Value-based healthcare payment models focus generally on optimizing the use of healthcare assets and services, and at present, specifically on reducing hospital admissions, readmissions, emergency department visits, observation unit stays, and ancillary services. These new payment models require that providers pay particular attention to the non-healthcare determinants of health. They require providers to develop inter-sectoral and transdisciplinary partnerships which align and apply the knowledge and resources of diverse communities to achieve desired health improvements.

The emerging value-based healthcare economy portends a fundamental change in how healthcare systems operate. In moving from 'volume to value', healthcare providers must better manage the care of their patient populations with chronic conditions and multiple co-morbidities, aggressively encourage health-promoting behaviors, and ensure care is provided in the most appropriate and least costly settings, which will often not be acute care settings. Success in this new paradigm requires that healthcare providers operationalize population health and population health management as core competencies.

III. Institute for Population Health Improvement—Overview

The Institute for Population Health Improvement (IPHI or the Institute) was founded as an independent operating unit within the University of California Davis Health System (UCDHS) in mid-2011 to operationalize a forward-looking vision about how the university might collaborate with California state government to improve population health by engaging in, developing, and promoting educational, research, and policy-related activities aimed at improving population health. The Institute was anticipated to develop and promote collaborations with government agencies (especially the California state government), as well as non-governmental and philanthropic organizations, focusing particularly on emerging issues in population and public health and innovative models of healthcare delivery that have the potential to improve population health.

The University of California Davis (UC Davis or UCD) is one of the thirteen campuses and national laboratories which comprise the University of California (UC) system, the nation's second largest academic system. UC Davis was founded as a land grant university in 1909. The main UC Davis campus is located in the town of Davis, about fifteen miles west of Sacramento; it is home to, among other notable assets, the world's number one ranked school of veterinary medicine. It is also the world's number one ranked university for agricultural and environmental sciences. The UC Davis School of Medicine and the Betty Irene Moore School of Nursing are located on the university's health sciences campus in Sacramento, about three miles from the state capital and the headquarters offices of all the state agencies.

Five primary strategic objectives have been pursued in operationalizing IPHI. These are to:

1 Provide thought leadership and nurture scholarship in population health
2 Develop and disseminate actionable health intelligence
3 Champion activities which strengthen health security and eliminate health disparities

4   Build health leadership capacity
5   Advocate for clinical and public health practices and policies which
    will improve population health

To actualize these strategic aims, the Institute has developed a tactical
programmatic foundation in five overlapping and mutually reinforcing
thematic areas: (1) data analytics and health intelligence, (2) quality
improvement, (3) public health practice, (4) health leadership development,
and (5) health policy.

The Institute is funded almost entirely from extramural sources. It has
no clinical activities, so it cannot generate clinical revenue, and it has no
connection with the UC Davis Medical Center per se. Beginning with no
extramural funds and one staff member, the Institute has grown to be a
well-functioning organization that has garnered more than $85 million in
total funding during its first five years of operation. Figure 9.1 displays
these funds according to thematic area. These funds have yielded over
$12 million in indirect cost recovery for the university and supported as
many as 127 full time employees (FTE). In the 2015–16 fiscal year the
Institute has a budget of approximately $12 million and 62 FTE.

In developing its programmatic portfolio the Institute has successfully
partnered with multiple governmental agencies and philanthropic

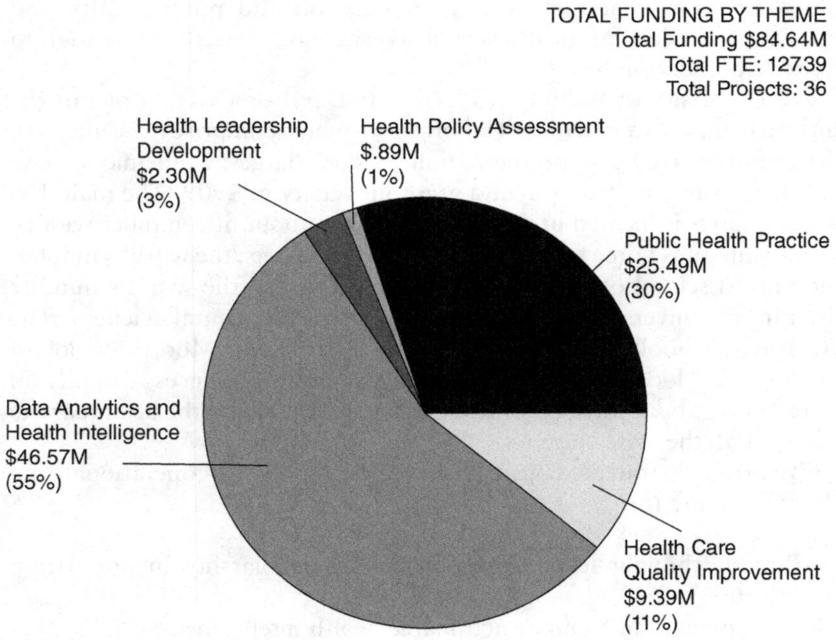

TOTAL FUNDING BY THEME
Total Funding $84.64M
Total FTE: 127.39
Total Projects: 36

Health Leadership
Development
$2.30M
(3%)

Health Policy Assessment
$.89M
(1%)

Public Health Practice
$25.49M
(30%)

Data Analytics and
Health Intelligence
$46.57M
(55%)

Health Care
Quality Improvement
$9.39M
(11%)

Figure 9.1 IPHI's Aggregate Funding by Thematic Area, FY 2012–2016

organizations, including the California Health and Human Services Agency (CHHSA), the California Departments of Health Care Services (DHCS), Public Health (CDPH), Housing and Community Development (DHCD), and Social Services (DSS), California Emergency Medical Services Authority (EMSA), California HealthCare Foundation (CHCF), the California Endowment (TCE), Robert Wood Johnson Foundation (RWJF), the Sierra Health Foundation (SHF), and the Hospital Quality Institute (HQI) of the California Hospital Association. IPHI has received one small cancer-related research grant from Genomic Health, Inc.

IV. IPHI Programmatic Activities

During its first five years of operation IPHI has engaged in thirty-four collaborations that have spanned a wide range of topics (see Table 9.1). Some of these projects are highlighted in the paragraphs below that discuss the IPHI's five tactical program areas.

A. Data Analytics and Health Intelligence

Through data analytics, the Institute seeks to create actionable health intelligence. Most notable among its activities in this regard are the California Cancer Reporting and Epidemiologic Surveillance Program and the Medi-Cal Quality Improvement Program, though several other projects categorized under other thematic areas also have required substantial data analytics.

The *California Cancer Reporting and Epidemiologic Surveillance (CalCARES) Program* manages the day-to-day operations of the California Cancer Registry (CCR), the nation's largest population-based state cancer registry and one of the largest cancer registries in the world. Since the statewide cancer registry was established in 1988, it has collected information on more than four million cancer patients. Nearly half of the data collected by the National Cancer Institute's Surveillance, Epidemiology, and End Results (SEER) program comes from the CCR.

CalCARES is funded by a five-year $28.9 million inter-agency agreement (IAA) with the California Department of Public Health (CDPH). The Institute assumed responsibility for the management and operations of the CCR in April 2012. While the CCR is operated by the CDPH, its day-to-day management has always been outsourced. Prior to 2012, the same contractor had performed this function since the statewide cancer registry was established in 1988. Transitioning the program from the previous contractor was a major administrative and logistical undertaking, involving hiring some fifty specialized staff and relocating office equipment and network servers while maintaining ongoing operations. This posed

Table 9.2 Programmatic Activities

Grant/Contract Name	Role	Funding Source	Amount	Funding Period
Medi-Cal Quality Improvement Program	PI	CDPH	$5,596,842	10/01/2011 to 09/30/2016
Evidence-based Policy Tools to Promote Health Policy and Disease Prevention	Co-PI	CDC	$150,000	01/02/2012 to 06/30/2013
High Risk Operating Room and Surgical Adverse Events and Prevention of Retained Surgical Items	PI	CDPH	$825,346	01/02/2012 to 06/30/2015
California Cancer Registry Program (effective January 1, 2014, the California Cancer Reporting and Epidemiologic Surveillance Program)	PI	CDPH	$28,963,840	04/01/2012 to 06/30/3017
Project LEAN	Co-PI	CDPH	$2,718,617	04/01/2012 to 06/30/2014
California Active Communities	PI	CDPH	$142,858	07/01/2012 to 06/30/2013
California Heart Disease and Stroke Prevention Program and California Arthritis Program	PI	CDPH	$3,861,042	07/01/2012 to 09/30/2014
California Tobacco Control Program	PI	CDPH	$8,879,270	07/01/2012 to 06/30/2017
Every Woman Counts Program	PI	DHCS	$1,425,758	07/01/2012 to 07/31/2014
California Health eQuality Program (ONC State Cooperative Agreement Health Information Exchange Development Program)	PI	CHHS	$16,582,100	09/01/2012 to 01/31/2014
Leveraging EMS Assets and Community Paramedicine	PI	CHCF	$104,878	07/23/2012 to 01/31/2014
Use of the OncoDx Assay Among California Breast Cancer Patients Covered by Medi-Cal	PI	Genomic Health, Inc.	$62,579	07/20/2012 to 07/19/2015
Sacramento Policy Briefings	PI	CHCF	$277,303	01/01/2013 to 12/31/2015
CDPH Accreditation Readiness Team Project	PI	CDPH	$499,675	03/01/2013 to 12/31/2013
CDPH Quality Improvement Training Project	PI	CDPH	$187,980	04/01/2013 to 05/01/2014

Project	Role	Funder	Amount	Period
Medi-Cal-Medicare Dual Eligibility Evaluation Program	PI	DHCS	$155,350	04/26/2013 to 08/25/2013
California State Innovations Model (CalSIM), CMS Innovations Planning Grant	PI	CHHS/CMS	$2,260,298	05/10/2013 to 03/31/2014
California Wise Women Program	PI	CDPH	$1,345,107	07/01/2013 to 06/30/2017
Adult Medicaid Quality Improvement Training	PI	DHCS/CMS	$158,619	11/01/2013 to 12/20/2014
California Health Policy Forum	PI	CHCF	$123,911	11/01/2013 to 12/31/2015
Design and Delivery of the Sierra Health Foundation Health Leadership Program	PI	Sierra Health Foundation	$124,861	11/01/2013 to 06/30/2015
Medi-Cal Data Symposium Series	PI	CHCF	$299,545	12/01/2013 to 12/15/2015
Laboratory LOINC Mapping Assistance Program	PI	CHCF	$425,000	02/01/2014 to 07/31/2015
CDPH Public Health Accreditation Program	PI	CDPH	$334,022	01/01/2014 to 09/30/2015
HQI/California Hospital Engagement Network Analytics	PI	Hospital Quality Institute	$202,526	05/01/2014 to 12/08/2014
Nutrition, Evaluation and Obesity Prevention Program Evaluation	PI	Public Health Institute	$179,955	03/01/2014 to 09/30/2014
HQI Analytics	PI	Hospital Quality Institute	$239,880	12/09/2014 to 12/08/2015
Travel Scholarship Program	PI	The California Endowment	$100,000	09/01/2013 to 12/31/2015
Licensing Standards for ASCs, CORFs, and Dialysis Clinics (California Senate Bill 534 Legislative Analysis)	PI	CDPH	$202,445	10/21/2014 to 09/30/2015
Mentored Research Scientist Development Program	Mentor	Robert Wood Johnson Foundation	$99,996	01/15/2014 to 01/14/2016
Sierra Health Leadership Program Years 2 and 3	PI	Sierra Health Foundation	$270,000	07/01/2015 to 06/30/2017
Obesity Prevention	PI	DHCS	$3,904,789	09/09/2015 to 09/30/2017
Veterans Housing and Homelessness Prevention Program	PI	California Department of Housing and Community Development	$150,000	09/30/2015 to 06/30/2016
EMS Core Measures	PI	EMSA	$40,000	04/01/2016 to 09/30/2016

substantial challenges, including creating a new administrative structure, physically moving to a new location, and adapting to a new business environment, but all major deliverables were met during the time period. This required extremely close collaboration between and among the Institute and the primary CCR stakeholders, including the CDPH, California's eight regional cancer registries, and various administrative support programs.

As part of its scope of work, CalCARES regularly produces annual and other periodic reports on the epidemiology of cancer in the state. CalCARES also supports a wide range of research conducted by investigators at numerous universities and research organizations across the nation. Since IPHI assumed management of the CCR, CalCARES has also promulgated a number of topical reports not required by the IAA's statement of work. These have included reports on infant cancers (Morris, Cook et al. 2014), obesity-related cancers (Cook et al. 2013), cancer stage at diagnosis (Morris et al. 2013), human papillomavirus associated cancers (Cook et al. ND), trends in cancer in California (Morris, Angel et al. 2014), and disparities in cancer care outcomes by source of health insurance (Parikh-Patel et al. 2015). Reports on colorectal cancer in Hispanic men and kidney cancer are presently being finalized.

The CalCARES program is currently pursuing a new collaboration to explore development of a "Population Health Integrated Data System for Cancer Control" using the CCR as the lynchpin of the system. This project seeks to assess the feasibility of linking diverse state health and healthcare, social service, and environmental data bases with the CCR to systematize transdisciplinary analyses of cancer occurrence and mortality. Conceptually, this builds on an earlier project which considered whether the CCR could be leveraged to improve clinical cancer care (Hiatt et al. 2015).

The *Medi-Cal Quality Improvement Program (MCQuIP)* was launched with a five-year $4.2 million inter-agency agreement with the California Department of Health Care Services (DHCS) in late 2011. The scope of the program was expanded and its budget augmented by $1.3 million in 2015. This program seeks to improve the quality of care provided by Medi-Cal, California's Medicaid program, and improve Medi-Cal members' overall health status. The DHCS recently engaged the Institute in an additional five-year $3.9 million collaboration focused on nutrition education and obesity prevention among Medi-Cal members and other low-income Californians.

Medi-Cal is the nation's largest Medicaid program and California's largest health insurer, having an annual budget of some $95 billion in 2015 and providing health insurance coverage for some 13.5 million Californians or about one third of the state's population, including half of all children. The MCQuIP was established during a period of unparalleled change for Medi-Cal and the DHCS. These changes have included an unprecedented expansion of Medi-Cal consequent to the Affordable Care Act, a wholesale shift in coverage of members from fee-for-service to managed care, implementation of a far-reaching Section 1115 Medicaid Waiver, and implementation of a large pilot project for joint coverage of Medicare-Medi-Cal dual eligible beneficiaries. Enrollment in Medi-Cal increased by over 4.5 million members since 2011 due to the Affordable Care Act.

Illustrative of the MCQuIP's work, in March 2015, in collaboration with the DHCS and California HealthCare Foundation, IPHI organized a substantially oversubscribed symposium on Medi-Cal high utilizers—i.e. the 5% of members who account for more than 50% of expenditures. This symposium was based on work done in the previous year and was the first time this information had been made available publicly. The symposium was sold out, and in an effort to meet the demand for the information a webinar on the same topic was held in June 2015; more than five hundred persons registered for the webinar.

B. Quality Improvement

IPHI's quality improvement (QI) activities have included both clinical and public health practices. Selected collaborations illustrate these efforts.

In 2012, IPHI launched a CDPH-funded project to evaluate reported surgical adverse events in California, since reporting of healthcare adverse events (aka "never events") was statutorily mandated in 2007. The project focused especially on trying to answer the important policy question of whether mandatory reporting of surgical adverse events has improved surgical practice and reduced the occurrence of preventable surgical errors. While the project generated a substantial amount of useable information, various data limitations precluded determining whether reporting has had a salutary effect on the occurrence of adverse surgical events at the population level. Multiple recommendations were made to CDPH for how adverse event investigation data might be standardized and augmented so that it could be used to answer the above noted policy question and for other population health purposes (Wu and Kizer 2015). In May 2015, IPHI organized a very well-attended statewide symposium based on this work to discuss the occurrence and prevention of surgical adverse events in California.

In another CDPH-funded project, we assessed quality of care issues in ambulatory surgical clinics, outpatient rehabilitation facilities, and renal dialysis clinics, and addressed the policy question of whether enhanced regulation would be likely to improve the quality of care provided at these facilities (Wu et al. 2015). As far as we could determine, this was the first time national information in this regard had been collated and analyzed.

During 2014–2015 IPHI worked with the non-profit Hospital Quality Institute (HQI) of the California Hospital Association to develop and execute a coordinated approach to acquiring, managing, and analyzing quality of care data collected from its member hospitals, focusing especially on data collected through the approximately 150 hospitals participating in the California *Hospital Engagement Network* funded by the federal Centers for Medicare and Medicaid Services (CMS). In 2015, IPHI assisted HQI in disseminating quality improvement and patient safety information throughout California; this included developing the *Hospital Consumer Assessment of Healthcare Providers and Systems (HCAHPS) Star Ratings Data Visualization Tool for California.* This internet-based interactive data visualization tool depicts Star Ratings of California hospitals based on CMS Hospital Compare and HCAHPS patient experience survey data (http://www.hcttf.org/releases/2015/1/28/major-health-care-players-unite-to-accelerate-transformation-of-us-health-care-system).

As part of the MCQuIP, IPHI conducted an assessment of health promotion interventions provided to members by Medi-Cal's 22 managed care plans (Backman et al. 2012). The results of this evaluation and recommendations for how managed care plans might improve the quality of these interventions are currently being utilized by the DHCS to improve health promotion services provided by Medi-Cal managed care plans.

The Institute has recently launched a new project with the California Emergency Medical Services Authority (EMSA) to assess reporting practices and use of emergency medical service (EMS) performance measures by local EMS agencies in the state. This follows a project completed for EMSA which assessed the feasibility of developing community paramedicine in California (Kizer et al. 2013). Among other findings of this latter project, the IPHI recommended EMSA pursue community paramedicine pilot projects in twelve communities at diverse locations in the state to develop 'real world' experiential information about this very promising model of community-based healthcare. Those pilot projects are currently underway.

In another QI-focused project, the IPHI enlisted the assistance of the UC Davis Extension Service to develop a three-hour internet-based quality improvement training module for use by all four thousand CDPH employees. Reportedly, this training has been enthusiastically received by both staff and management. The training module is additionally being used by California's local public health departments as a component toward obtaining national accreditation. (In an unrelated project, IPHI assisted the CDPH in becoming one of the first state public health departments in the nation to receive national accreditation.)

C. Public Health Practice

The Institute's areas of focus within public health practice have included tobacco control, heart disease and stroke prevention, arthritis, nutrition and obesity prevention, cancer screening, and implementing health information technology and health information exchanges.

In 2012 the IPHI entered into a three-year $6.0 million IAA with the CDPH to support the state's internationally acclaimed Tobacco Control Program. The California Tobacco Control Program (CTCP) seeks to reduce illness and preventable deaths attributable to the use of tobacco products. The CTCP partners with local health agencies and nonprofit community-based organizations in all fifty-eight counties to fund and coordinate local community activities to create smoke-free environments, prevent illegal sales of tobacco products to youth, counter the aggressive marketing practices of the tobacco industry, and help smokers quit. The CTCP's approach to changing social norms to create a tobacco-free environment is considered an international 'best practice' model (Tobacco Control Section 1998). The IPHI works closely with the CDPH to implement this model program. The Institute's agreement with the CDPH was extended for two years and augmented by an additional $2.8 million in 2015.

Also in 2012, the Institute entered into a $2.7 million agreement to manage *Project LEAN*, a nutrition and obesity prevention program, a $143,000 agreement to manage the *California Active Communities Program* physical activity promotion initiative, a $3.9 million agreement to manage the *California Heart Disease and Stroke Prevention Program* and the *California Arthritis Program*, and a $1.4 million agreement to manage the *Every Woman Counts Program*, a cancer screening and early detection program for low income women. Notwithstanding the Department's satisfaction with IPHI's performance, at the end of FY 2013–14 the CDPH did not renew these IAAs consequent to a change in state policy which resulted in these programs being brought 'in house' and administered by state government employees. This type of rather abrupt and nonperformance-related change is an inherent risk in these types of collaborations.

Further, in September 2012 the Institute entered into a sixteen-month $16.6 million agreement with the California Health and Human Services Agency (CHHSA) to launch the *California Health eQuality (CHeQ) Program*. Briefly in the way of background, in April 2012 California's Secretary of Health and Human Services queried whether IPHI might be willing to assume management of the *Office of the National Coordinator for Health Information Technology (ONC) State Cooperative Agreement for Health Information Exchange Development*. California had been awarded a $39 million four-year ONC state cooperative agreement in 2010. The Legislature established an entity (Cal e-Connect) to implement the award; however, after more than two years, and with nearly $20 million expended, the CHHSA was concerned about the slowness with which the program was being implemented and the paucity of tangible outcomes. The CHHSA opted to change management of the cooperative agreement and tasked the IPHI with the responsibility for managing the remainder of the cooperative agreement (Raths 2012). IPHI considered this to be a high-risk endeavor because of the many challenges of taking on such a large and complicated program so 'late in the game'.

The CHeQ Program required a very rapid ramp-up. Twenty-one staff members needed to be newly hired or transferred from Cal-e-Connect to UC Davis positions, and more than twenty individual contracts and subcontracts needed to be executed very quickly. These rapid response needs materially stressed the university's human resources and contracts management infrastructure. However, by working together very closely and collaboratively we were able to smoothly transition selected elements of Cal e-Connect and develop a new, outcomes-focused program. A great deal was accomplished through the CHeQ Program, with all but $1 million of the allotted funds being expended by the end of the cooperative agreement (California Health and Human Services Agency 2014; Edlin 2013). The ONC state cooperative agreements were one-time grants which were not eligible for extension or renewal; California's agreement ended in January 2014.

Additionally, in the area of health information exchange, since conducting an assessment of the feasibility of establishing a health information exchange in Los Angeles for the chief executive officer of Los Angeles County and the Los Angeles County Board of Supervisors in 2009, through IPHI I have served on the governing board of the *Los Angeles Network for Enhanced Services (LANES)*, which seeks to establish a HIE for the greater Los Angeles area. The original LANES public-private partnership has evolved into a non-profit, public benefit corporation. The LANES HIE began selected operations in 2015. When fully operational LANES will be the largest HIE in the world.

Another highly challenging collaboration occurred in 2013, when we entered into a six-month $2.3 million agreement to assist the CHHSA develop a proposal for a *CMS State Innovations Model (CalSIM) CMS Innovations Planning Grant* aimed at cultivating innovative models of delivering healthcare in California. Again, this program required a very rapid ramp-up entailing the execution of multiple time-sensitive personnel actions and contracts. While the agreement was ultimately extended by four months, extraordinary efforts were required at times to successfully execute this agreement. A $100 million grant proposal was successfully prepared and submitted, although it was not funded by CMS.

In 2013 the Institute entered into a four-year $1.3 million collaboration with the CDPH to support the Well-Integrated Screening and Evaluation for Women Across the Nation (WISEWOMAN) program. Administered by the federal Centers for Disease Control and Prevention (CDC), the WISEWOMAN program seeks to eliminate racial and ethnic health disparities by screening low-income, uninsured, or under-insured women aged 40 to 64 years of age for heart disease and stroke risk factors. CDC funds twenty-one WISEWOMAN programs in nineteen states, three of which are in California.

As a result of multiple large IAAs ending in 2014 the Institute sustained a major reduction in funding that year, making it necessary to reduce staffing by some fifty FTEs. These types of funding swings are inherent to the nature of the Institute's work and necessitate maintaining personnel management practices that are as flexible as possible. The university's human resource policies and practices have presented substantial challenges in this regard, but by working very closely with the UC Davis Human Resources staff these and other situations have been successfully managed.

The IPHI has continually sought to broaden the scope of its public health practice partnerships. Illustrative of this, in FY 2015–16 a project was launched with the California Department of Housing and Community Development, in collaboration with the California Housing Finance Authority and the California Department of Veterans Affairs, to assist with implementation of the voter-approved $600 million Veterans Housing and Homelessness Prevention (VHHP) Bond Act of 2014, Proposition 41 (https://ballotpedia.org/California_Proposition_41,_Veterans_Housing_and_Homeless_Prevention_Bond). While the VHHP Program is a small collaboration from a funding perspective, it has significant potential for addressing a serious public health problem—i.e. homelessness among veterans.

Finally, as part of the Medi-Cal Quality Improvement Program IPHI and DHCS collaborated in 2014 to develop *Welltopia™ the place of wellness*, a website that provides reliable health and wellness information for beneficiaries of state-funded programs and other underserved populations (http://mywelltopia.com). Funds to establish the Welltopia™ website were made available from the CHeQ Program. In September 2015 Welltopia™ was awarded the 2015 Digital Government Achievement Award (DGAA) from GovTech's Center for Digital Government.

D. Health Leadership Development

In 2014, after a competitive process, the Institute was selected by the Sierra Health Foundation to re-launch the foundation's Health Leadership Program (HLP) after a two-year hiatus. The HLP is a nine-month executive style leadership development program for leaders of non-profit community-based organizations and local government agencies in inland northern California. The HLP was formerly managed by the University of Southern California's Sacramento Center. IPHI has partnered with Dr. Richard Callahan, Chairman of the Department of Public and Nonprofit Administration at the University of San Francisco, to manage this program. Since making the initial one-year award, the SHF renewed the agreement with IPHI for two years, and expanded it to include provision of continued leadership development training for alumni of the program. Additional health leadership collaborations are currently being discussed.

E. Health Policy

For the past three years the Institute has managed the *California Health Policy Forum*, the *Medi-Cal Data Symposium Series*, and *Sacramento Policy Briefings* funded by the California HealthCare Foundation and, for the latter, the California Endowment. Some of the topics presented at these forums are listed in Table 9.2. Likewise, the IPHI has organized various symposia and webinars aimed at promoting population health; representative examples of these are shown in Table 9.3.

In 2012 a representative of the IPHI served as a member of the *Let's Get Healthy California Task Force* established by Executive Order B-19-12, issued by Governor Jerry Brown on May 3, 2012. The Task Force was charged to "develop a ten-year plan for improving the health of Californians, controlling health care costs, promoting personal responsibility for health, and advancing health equity", with the overall purpose of making California the healthiest state in the nation by 2022 (Office of the Governor 2012).

Table 9.2 IPHI Organized Health Policy Forums and Briefings, 2013–2015

Date	Subject/Title
January 30, 2013	Data Match: Streamlining Eligibility and Enrollment Under the Affordable Care Act
February 12, 2013	The Status of the Implementation of Medi-Cal Mental Health Services
March 26, 2013	Chronic Disease Prevention: The Social Equity Lens
March 28, 2013	Transitioning the SPD Population to Medi-Cal Managed Care: Examining the Experiences of Beneficiaries
May 8, 2013	Closing the Gap: Ending Variation in End-of-Life Care in California
August 6, 2013	Enabling Information Among California Health Providers
September 27, 2013	Payment Reform: Changing How We Pay for Health Care
October 30, 2013	Bringing Greater Transparency to Cancer Care in California

Date	Subject/Title
December 9, 2013	Inside the Black Box: The Future of Price Transparency in California
December 17, 2013	Monitoring Performance: A Dashboard of Medi-Cal Managed Care
April 14, 2014	In Their Own Words: Consumers' and Enrollment Counselors' Experiences with Covered California
October 1, 2014	Maternity Care in California: Status Update and Opportunities for Improvement
October 16, 2014	Monitoring Access to Care for Medi-Cal Enrollees in a Time of Change
November 14, 2014	Enabling California Cancer Registry to Measure and Improve Care
December 3, 2014	Exploring the need for a POLST Registry in California
July 29, 2015	Making Information Available on Outpatient Surgery in California
December 10, 2015	ACA's Impact on Medi-Cal Managed Care Plans and Safety-Net Clinics

Table 9.3 Representative IPHI Symposia and Webinars, 2014–2015

Date	Subject/Title
March 10, 2014	Using Performance Measures to Improve Quality webinar. Medicaid Adult Quality Measures Grantee States[1]
June 19, 2014	Using Data to Improve Maternity Care in California: Research Collaborations and Future Opportunities[2]
March 4, 2015	Understanding High Utilizers of Medi-Cal Services; California HealthCare Foundation[2]
April 1, 2015	Restructuring a State Nutrition Education and Obesity Prevention Program: Implications of a Local Health Department Model webinar[3]
May 14–15, 2015	Eliminating Serious Patient Safety Events in Surgical and Procedural Areas: A Statewide Conference and Call to Action for California Hospitals[4]
May 27, 2015	The Rise and Fall of VA Healthcare: 1994–2014 webinar[5]
June 6, 2015	Understanding Medi-Cal High Utilizers webinar[2]

[1] Funded and organized by Academy Health
[2] Funded by the California HealthCare Foundation
[3] Funded and organized by the Robert Wood Johnson Foundation, Public Health Services and Systems Research Program
[4] Funded by the California Department of Public Health
[5] Funded and organized by the American College of Preventive Medicine

Further, the IPHI, in collaboration with the Institute for Health Policy Studies at the University of California San Francisco, co-mentored a Commonwealth Fund-sponsored Harkness International Fellow in Health Policy and Innovation in 2013–2014. A report on some of the mentee's work was published in the *Journal of Health Policy, Politics and Law* in 2015 (Murphy et al. 2015). This was the first time that UC Davis ever participated in this prestigious international health policy program. Similarly, in 2014 the IPHI received a Robert Wood Johnson Foundation-funded *Mentored Research Scientist Development Award*, which is part of the RWJF's *Public Health Systems and Services Research Program*. Again, this was the first time UC Davis ever participated in this highly competitive program.

F. Integrative Medicine Program

The IPHI is also home to the UC Davis Integrative Medicine Program (IMP). The program works to prevent and control lifestyle-related conditions such as arteriosclerotic heart disease, hypertension, type 2 diabetes, and obesity. It does this by facilitating the adoption of healthful habits in the areas of nutrition, exercise, stress management, and tobacco use. Its primary focus has been in promoting plant-based diets as the principal means of preventing, halting the progression of, and reversing chronic conditions. The IMP has developed a very successful content-driven online and social media strategy to reach the general population. In the last twelve months the IMP had almost three million individual readers of its blog, experienced more than 1000% growth in its social media follower base, and added more than 22,000 people to its mailing list. The IMP has also sponsored a three-week online 'food challenge' to coach over 10,000 people all over the world on how to adopt and follow a plant-based diet.

V. Challenges

During its first five years the Institute has encountered a number of challenges. These have included the challenges incumbent to any organizational start-up, as well as some stemming from 'pushing' the university to operate in unaccustomed ways. As briefly noted in preceding sections, some of these challenges have required exceptional efforts to resolve.

The Institute's primary challenges can be divided into three categories: human resource and contracting issues; achieving long-term financial sustainability; and internal UC Davis collaborations.

A. Human Resource and Contracting Issues

The university's personnel and contracting processes have proven to be problematic when launching programs requiring rapid implementation and quick ramp-ups, as collaborative efforts often do. This was particularly so with the CalCARES, CHeQ, and CalSIM Planning Grant projects, three of the Institute's largest projects. Unfortunately, the logistical problems experienced with the latter two of these agreements have reportedly discouraged the CHHSA from further contracting with the Institute. Along the same lines, several of IPHI's partners have opined that UC Davis is more difficult to work with than other UC campuses. In several instances the Institute has been advised that while it would have been the preferred programmatic partner the funding organization decided to partner with another UC campus or a private university or organization because of less cumbersome personnel and contracting processes. It is unclear why there seem to be significant differences in these practices among the UC campuses.

Additionally, most of the Institute's programs require working closely with state agency staff and substantial amounts of service work, things which university faculty members may not be accustomed to doing (or at least, not to the degree required). In a couple instances, non-IPHI faculty members who have been engaged to work on our projects have found it difficult to adjust to the project needs. In one case, after repeated counseling of the individual, the sponsoring organization determined it needed a different consultant.

B. Achieving Long-Term Financial Sustainability

The Institute has worked hard to expand its partnership portfolio and diversify its funding base. Broad state policy decisions have at times undermined these efforts, as occurred in 2014. The above described contracting and human resource management challenges have also confounded the Institute's efforts to some degree. We have found little interest among local government agencies in partnering with the Institute, or academic institutions generally, because of the typically higher overhead costs at universities compared to private organizations. Since project personnel often work on-site at the sponsoring organization, these organizations sometimes find it difficult to justify paying the university's indirect cost recovery rate. Nonetheless, the Institute continues to work to develop long-term partnerships with state agencies, as well as to strategize on how to obtain funding from non-government sources—especially philanthropic organizations—that will enhance the government collaborations.

C. UC Davis Health System (UCDHS) and School of Medicine (SOM) Collaboration

IPHI has successfully developed many government and external partnerships and collaborations; however, similar collaborations within the UC Davis Health System have not matured despite multiple efforts to cultivate such relationships. Recognizing the Institute's substantial expertise in population health management, quality improvement, and patient safety, and the relevant work it has been doing for other entities, the lack of engagement by the UCDHS has been puzzling in light of the needs of the population (UCDHS) serves. The lack of engagement seems to be largely driven by the health system's ambivalence, at least to date, about population health management and value-based payment. Nonetheless, developing collaborative relationships with the health system for population health improvement will remain an ongoing priority for the Institute.

VI. The Future

Going forward, the Institute will build on the foundation that has been developed during its first five years, expanding and diversifying the funding base and scope of activities. It will continue to explore new collaborations with existing partners, and seek to develop new relationships with other population health-related government agencies, philanthropies, and community organizations.

One specific potential opportunity which the Institute plans to explore in the near term will be collaborations with health insurers and large cancer care providers. Recognizing the magnitude of the cost of cancer care, the substantial opportunities for improving cancer care, and the growing prevalence of cancer patients, among other things, we believe payers and providers will increasingly seek to better manage their populations of cancer patients in response to the emerging value-based healthcare economy. CalCARES provides a means for jumpstarting such efforts, utilizing, among other things, the groundwork done in preparing the 2015 report, *Disparities in Stage at Diagnosis, Survival, and Quality of Care in California by Source of Health Insurance* (Parikh-Patel et al. 2015).

The Institute also hopes to materially expand its nascent *Center for Veterans and Military Health (CVMH)*, capitalizing on the IPHI leadership's extensive footprint in veterans' health issues and the work it is doing with the Veterans Housing and Homelessness Prevention Program. The CVMH was launched in 2013, following multiple conversations with the leadership of the Northern California VA Health Care System (NCVAHCS) and Travis Air Force Base (TAFB), but the momentum for advancing the center lessened under new leadership at both NCVAHCS and TAFB. The effort went dormant in 2015. However, implementing the agreement for the VHHP and present efforts to develop a multi-sectoral collaboration to serve vision-impaired veterans in northern California offer an opportunity to resurrect the CVMH. The Institute leadership believes there are significant opportunities for partnerships with philanthropic and veteran service organizations to improve veterans' health.

A number of other collaborations are also being explored, including a potentially fertile opportunity in the evolving focus on population and planetary health. Interest in this topical area has materially increased since the publication of the Rockefeller Foundation-Lancet Commission report on planetary health in the summer of 2015 (Whitmee et al. 2015). In light of UC Davis' well-recognized expertise in veterinary medicine, agriculture and environmental sciences, primary care, and public health the Institute leadership believes that there is an unparalleled opportunity to develop population and planetary health collaborations at UC Davis.

References

Backman D.R., N.D. Kohatsu, B.M. Paciotti, J.V. Byrne, and K.W. Kizer. 2012. Health promotion interventions for low-income Californians through Medi-Cal managed care plans. *Preventing Chronic Disease.* 12(11, E196); 1–11.

Berwick D.M., T.M. Nolan and J. Whittington. 2008. The triple aim: Care, health and cost. *Health Affairs* 27(3):759–69.

Burwell, S.M. 2015. Setting value-based payment goals—HHS efforts to improve U.S. health care. *N Engl J Med.* 372(10): 897–9.

California Health and Human Services Agency. 2014. *California HIE Landscape 2013.* Sacramento, CA.

Cook S.N., B.M. Giddings, A. Parikh-Patel, K.W. Kizer, J.H. Bates, and K.P. Snipes. 2013. *Obesity-Linked Cancers: A California Status Report, 1988–2009.* Sacramento, CA: California Department of Public Health.

Cook S.N., B.M. Giddings, C.R. Morris, et al. (ND) *Human Papillomavirus (HPV)-Associated Cancers and HPV Vaccination Coverage in California.* Sacramento, CA: California Department of Public Health, Chronic Disease Surveillance and Research Branch.

Edlin, M. 2013. Health Information Exchange Taking Root in Northern California. *CaliforniaHealthline.* December 2.

Health Care Transformation Task Force. 2015. Major health care players unite to accelerate transformation of U.S. health care system. http://www.hcttf.org/releases/2015/1/28/major-health-care-players-unite-to-accelerate-transformation-of-us-health-care-system (Accessed May 3, 2016).

Hiatt R.A., C.G. Tai, D.W. Blayney, et al. 2015. Leveraging state cancer registries to measure and improve the quality of cancer care: A potential strategy for California and beyond. *Journal of the National Cancer Institute.* 107(5); published online March 12, 2015.

Hospital Consumer Assessment of Healthcare Providers and Systems (HCAHPS) Star Ratings Data Visualization Tool for California. 2014. http://www.

hqinstitute.org/post/hcahps-star-ratings-data-visualizationtool-california. August 24. Accessed May 10, 2016.

Institute of Medicine. 2013. *U.S. Health in International Perspective: Shorter Lives, Poorer Health.* Washington, DC: National Academies Press.

Kizer K.W., K. Shore, and A. Moulin. 2013. *Community Paramedicine: A Promising Model for Integrating Emergency and Primary Care.* Sacramento, CA: Institute for Population Health Improvement, University of California, Davis.

Morris C.R., E. Angel, R. Martinsen, S. Cook, A. Parikh-Patel, and K.W. Kizer. 2014. *Trends in Cancer Incidence and Mortality in California, 1988–2010.* Sacramento, CA: California Cancer Reporting and Epidemiologic Surveillance Program, Institute for Population Health Improvement, University of California, Davis.

Morris C.R., S. Cook, A. Parikh-Patel, and K.W. Kizer. 2014. *Infant Cancers in California, 1988-2011.* Sacramento, CA. California Cancer Reporting and Epidemiologic Surveillance Program, Institute for Population Health Improvement, University of California, Davis.

Morris C.R., C.N. Ramirez, S.N. Cook, A. Parikh-Patel, K.W. Kizer, J.H. Bates, and K.P. Snipes. 2013. *Cancer Stage at Diagnosis.* Sacramento, CA. California Department of Public Health, Cancer Surveillance Section.

Murphy J., M. Ko, K.W. Kizer, and A.B. Bindman. 2015. Safety-net integration: A shared strategy for becoming providers of choice. *Journal of Health Politics, Policy and Law* 40 (2):403–419.

Office of the Governor. 2012. *Let's Get Healthy California Task Force Final Report.* Sacramento, CA. December 19.

Parikh-Patel A., C.R. Morris, R. Martinsen, and K.W. Kizer. 2015. *Disparities in Stage at Diagnosis, Survival, and Quality of Cancer Care in California by Source of Health Insurance.* Sacramento, CA. Institute for Population Health Improvement, University of California, Davis.

Proposition 41. 2014. https://ballotpedia.org/California_Proposition_41,_Veterans_Housing_and_Homeless_Prevention_Bond_(2014) (Accessed May 10, 2016)

Quality, Licensing, and Certification Program, California Department of Public Health. ND. Sacramento, CA. Institute for Population Health Improvement, University of California, Davis. http://www.cdph.ca.gov/programs/LnC/Pages/lnc.aspx. (accessed May 10, 2016)

Raths D. 2012. California Shifts HIE Leadership. *Healthcare Informatics.* May 2.

Squires D. and C. Anderson. 2015. *U.S. Health Care from a Global Perspective: Spending, Use of Services, Prices, and Health in 13 Countries.* New York, NY: The Commonwealth Fund.

Tobacco Control Section. 1998. *Model for Change: The California Experience in Tobacco Control.* Sacramento, CA: California Department of Health Services. October.

Welltopia. http://mywelltopia.com (Accessed May 3, 2016)

Whitmee S. et al. 2015. Safeguarding human health in the Anthropocene epoch: Report of the Rockefeller Foundation-Lancet Commission on planetary health. *Lancet* 386: 1793–2028.

Whittington J.W., K. Nolan, N. Lewis and T. Torres. 2015. Pursuing the triple aim: The first 7 years. *The Milbank Quarterly* 93(2): 263–300.

Wu, H., and K.W. Kizer. 2016. *Surgical Adverse Events in California: Trends in State Reporting and Recommendations for Prevention. Final Report to the Center for Health Care Quality, Licensing & Certification Program; California Department of Public Health.* Sacramento, CA. Institute for Population Health Improvement, University of California, Davis. In press.

Wu H.W., E. Montgomery, and K.W Kizer. 2015. *A Review of Regulatory Standards, Quality of Care Concerns, and Oversight of Ambulatory Surgery Clinics, End-Stage Renal Disease Facilities, and Comprehensive Outpatient Rehabilitation Facilities Final Report Prepared for the Center for Health Care Quality, Licensing & Certification Program; California Department of Public Health.* Sacramento, CA. Institute for Population Health Improvement, University of California, Davis.

10 Community Health Councils, Inc.

A Case Study in Addressing Health Inequities

Lavonna Blair Lewis, PhD, MPH

I. Dedication

The Community Health Councils, Inc. (CHC, Inc.) is a non-profit community-based, consumer-oriented health advocacy, education, and resource development organization. Established in response to the 1992 civil unrest in Los Angeles, CHC, Inc. strives to increase access to quality healthcare and improve the health status of uninsured, underinsured, and economically disadvantaged communities. This is accomplished through coalition building at the local and state level, consumer education, technical assistance training, and policy and leadership forums for community-based organizations. With deep roots in South Los Angeles—formerly South Central Los Angeles, but renamed in April 2003 with a Los Angeles City Council vote—CHC has responded to decades of neglect in the community through a concentrated focus on residents' health and the need for more health-supportive environments.

Kawachi et al. (2002) eloquently state: "inequality and equality are dimensional concepts, simply referring to measureable quantities. Inequity and equity, on the other hand, are political concepts, expressing a moral commitment to social justice." This chapter is dedicated to the memory and legacy of Lark Galloway Gilliam, a champion for social justice in all its forms, but most notably health equity. As the first Executive Director of Community Health Councils, Inc., Lark was a visionary leader and change agent, who over the course of more than two decades led a series of efforts to transform South Los Angeles and surrounding communities, from the ground up. Taking advantage of a myriad of policy windows (Kingdon 1995), she helped CHC and its collaborative partners develop a strong, coherent voice for change, impacting local and state elected officials and organizations, federal agencies, and ultimately national policy. While the argument presented here is not that CHC under Lark's leadership can claim credit for all the changes that have taken place in the City of Los Angeles in relation to health, the built environment, or policy and systems changes, it can certainly be argued that they, and she played a key role.

II. Introduction

The issue of ethnic and racial disparities in health is complex and multi-dimensional. The disparity is embedded within the inter-relationship and dynamic between the issues of racism, culture, and the economic structure that defines the experience of African American and other racial and ethnic groups in this country. Together these social issues represent the primary risk factors and the root causes behind the various physiological and behavioral risk factors traditionally associated with disease. However, issues of racism, culture, and economics are too often ignored by the medical and public health community. Consequently, interventions have traditionally addressed physiological and behavioral risk factors. However, by ignoring the social and economic reality of a population, there can be no long-term improvement in the health status of the community.

Fortunately, awareness of the need to understand the socioeconomic and cultural factors of an ethnic community and their impact on health has grown dramatically recently. It is increasingly apparent that the problems of chronic medical conditions, such as cardiovascular disease, diabetes, and cancers, cannot be fully explained by biomedical or genetic approaches. Much of the research based on community approaches has shown that health disparities among communities, associated with socioeconomic and ethnic marginalization, contribute to such medical conditions, and it has become the subject of increasing national attention from policy makers. It is well accepted that underserved communities with limited nutritional and physical activity resources have many obstacles that prevent residents from sustaining a healthy lifestyle. Particularly, communities with a high proportion of African Americans provide a stark example of the link between community environments and the onset of medical conditions such as cardiovascular disease or diabetes.

Based on this understanding, in Los Angeles the Community Health Councils, Inc. (CHC), a community-based non-profit health advocacy organization, began coalition building in 1998 to bring together organizations and individuals to combat health disparities around cardiovascular disease, hypertension, and diabetes within African American and other under-resourced communities in Los Angeles. Over time, these coalitions have provided a unique opportunity for researchers, public health experts, and community representatives to build a collective understanding and knowledge of the degree of health disparities, and to go beyond the symptoms and examine the root cause of the prevalence of disease and the barriers to health in underserved communities.

From the beginning, the project work has been designed and conducted through a community-based participatory research approach. Community-based participatory research (CBPR) is built on the concept that health promotion research should be conducted in a manner that allows community members to influence and control decisions that affect them and their community. Thus, CBPR is a partnership approach to research that equitably involves community members, organizational representatives, and researchers in all aspects of the research process, and recognizes the unique strengths that each brings. This research paradigm reflects an evolution in the scientific literature on community health interventions from benevolent paternalism to "community-based" interventions, to the more recent call for "community-directed" interventions.

Ethnic groups such as African Americans that have been socio-economically marginalized and disfranchised have a particular claim for involvement in the direction of research ostensibly designed to address problems in their communities. African Americans have good reason to distrust medical and public health researchers. CBPR provides a process model that, if instituted appropriately, elicits the trust of residents by responding to perceived community needs. Researchers and community members can develop a true partnership that builds community capacity by training residents in research skills, involving them in decision-making processes, and engaging them in change activities. Community research partnerships respond to community needs and culture rather than imposing a preconceived idea of what would help the community.

In these projects, individual behaviors were put into perspective by a new focus on the economic and social structure in a community that supports such behaviors. The question was not: do people have the will to change? Instead, it became: did people's environments encourage or discourage a healthy lifestyle? Changing the environment, it is argued, should over time result in new opportunities for healthy behavior. Defining and describing community residents' environments, then, became crucial, since knowing the environment, partly by documenting its assets and liabilities for health-promoting behaviors, allows for the development of targeted interventions that would create richer, more supportive environments for healthy living.

As a way to distinguish this assessment approach to community needs, the term "resource environment" (Sloane et al. 2003, 2006; Lewis et al. 2005, 2011) was used to identify the interactive and overlapping issues of accessibility, cost, and quality. Each community or neighborhood is intrinsically situated within a series of resource environments for healthcare, physical activity, nutrition, and other components that shape a community and influence the lives of its residents. Each of these resource environments is a network of institutions that residents depend upon to fulfill a specific need, such as the provision of healthcare services or access to non-fat milk. Each resource environment shapes the institutional or organizational "neighborhood" in which residents live, creating opportunities or challenges for residents making healthy decisions. Over time, the assessments of the resource environments through CBPR would not only provide a means of addressing economic and racial disparities in the community's health, but also led to policy and systems change interventions to promote health and attack the root causes of diseases. The remaining sections of this chapter begin with the current iteration of the CHC Model for Social Change, the result of almost twenty years' worth of CDC funding for multiple REACH initiatives. This will be followed by discussions of two rounds of REACH funding—a general overview of REACH 2010, which ran from 1999–2007, and a more detailed review of REACH US, which ran from 2007–2012, also the period of the most effective policy and systems change work.

III. The End from the Beginning: The Community Health Council Model for Social Change

Figure 10.1 summarizes the CHC Model for Community Change, which is rooted in the values of social justice, equity, and self-determination that support community empowerment in vulnerable communities. The CHC Model has involved a dynamic, building process, using the knowledge gained from past interventions and innovations introduced in 1998 and tested since 1999 to further refine the various approaches to advancing health equity. Below, we define and elaborate the various stages of the Model and how it maps onto the socio-ecological model's four levels of change.

The CHC Model builds upon the socio-ecological model's four levels of change (McLeroy et al. 1988; CDC 2015). At the first level are actions that seek to transform the individuals' behavior, knowledge, and understanding. Here, the focus would be on providing various stakeholders with information they could use to take steps to improve individual health behavior. The second level considers "a person's closest social circle— peers, partners and family members". Here, through various networks participants would be asked to share project-related information with the various individuals in their personal networks, to expand the impact of the project. A third level "explores the community settings, such as schools, workplaces, and neighborhoods, in which social relationships occur and seeks to identify the characteristics of these settings". Actions at this level focus on the infrastructure that would establish a platform for making healthy choices—the vendors, community organizations, elected officials, and their interaction with relevant populations of interest.

Finally, the societal level consists of factors that "create social and cultural norms", including "the health, economic, educational and social policies that help to maintain economic or social inequalities between groups in society". Reforms to policies and systems attempt to eliminate barriers to the resources needed to sustain a healthy community. The persistence and impact of institutional and structural racism on the health of racial and ethnic communities continue to limit success at the societal level. More analysis is needed to examine the extent to which the practices, policies, and systems for the allocation of resources create advantages

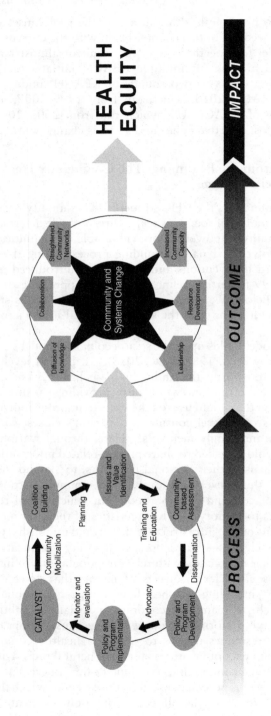

Figure 10. 1 Community Health Council Model for Community Change

based on race. The CHC Model works not only to identify how systems and policies affect populations inequitably, but also to develop strategies to combat these inequities.

A. The CHC Model and Community Change Process

The Catalyst: A catalyst is generally an individual, event, infusion of resources, or the right information at the right time to "provoke or speed significant change of action". The catalyst focuses and leverages the community's capabilities and assets to effect change. As the CHC-led coalitions transitioned between the levels, the experience and knowledge gained from past activities served as a catalyst for the next stage of project development.

Coalition Building: Berkowitz and Wolff (1988) define community coalitions as groups "involving multiple sectors of the community, coming together to address community needs and solve community problems". The formation and sustainability of a diverse community resident, local vendor, elected official, and practitioner coalition was foundational for the CHC Model. The coalition was the essential vehicle for engaging the impacted community and leading the bottom-up community change efforts. The coalition membership changed over time and activities, as the community developed its capacity and voice to lead broader policy and systems change efforts. Repeatedly, it was made clear that the parties recognized the strengths and assets of others and the increased leveraging opportunities that resulted from working together, especially in underserved and under-resourced communities.

Issues and Goal Identification: The coalition-building process begins with the identification and articulation of shared goals. Their identification does not necessitate agreement or alignment on every issue. The process engages stakeholders at each step to expand the depth of their understanding as well as develop "ownership" of the proposed activities. The development of a community action plan (CAP) serves as a tool for building consensus around the activities as well as defining the research question, strategy, and approach.

Community Assessment: An assessment by the community of its own resource and built environment is essential. The central principle of the assessment process is that the community partners work collaboratively at every stage of the assessment, from deciding what resources will be assessed to how the resulting data will be analyzed and disseminated. The approach allows CHC and its partners to use these assessments as a vehicle for building community awareness, community capacity, and ultimately policy advocacy.

Policy and Program Development: The development and articulation of the policy and/or program is based on the analysis of the community assessments. The strategy is examined from the vantage point of multiple stakeholders to ensure appropriateness and relevancy in connecting the problem to possible solutions.

Policy/Program Implementation and Evaluation: Denhardt states that policy implementation is the action phase of the policy-making process. Once plans have been made and policies decided upon, one must put them into operation. For the CHC Model, policy implementation is the opportunity to craft assessment data into policy advocacy tools. The multi-discipline composition of the coalition strengthens the potential for successful policy implementation by ensuring that all facets of the issue are taken into account.

Table 10. 1 CHC Model Stages in Relationship to Socio-Economic Model Levels

Stage	Individual and Relationship Levels	Community Level	Societal Level
Catalyst	CHC and REACH 2010 and REACH US Funding; CVD and diabetes disparities	Assessment data; insufficient nutrition resources	Assessment data; policy barriers to grocery store development
Coalition	Broad-based community and public health; enrollment of impacted population	Inclusion of grocery store owners and redevelopment agency	Multi-disciplinary including policy makers
Issue Identification	Morbidity/mortality/ obesity rates; lack of access to healthy nutrition	Lack of new store development; abundance of fast food restaurants w/ high calorie, low nutrient foods	Non-regulation of food retail density (grocery, convenient stores/fast food restaurant)
Community Assessment	Community assessment of food resource environment using community researchers; consumer focus groups.	Grocery store focus groups; findings dissemination	Findings dissemination to policy makers
Policy/Program Development	Health education curriculum; food demonstrations; coalition deliberation of policy recommendations	City Retail Marketing; finance and planning incentives to attract food retailers	City moratorium on development of fast food restaurants
Policy/Program Implementation and Evaluation	Neighborhood Food Watch campaign to raise consumer awareness and expectation regarding food access and quality	Grocery store/ sit-down restaurant incentive package	Incorporate food retail density regulations within Community Plan Update

The catalyst, composition of the coalition, definition of the issue, and intervention strategies change as we progress through the levels of the socio-ecological model on which this project focuses. The application of the CHC Model to each level of change is summarized in Table 10.1.

IV. The REACH 2010 Project from 1998–2007

The Racial and Ethnic Approaches to Community Health (REACH) 2010 Project was a national demonstration project managed by the Centers for Disease Control and Prevention. The project was developed to support the two-fold goals for Healthy People 2010:

- To increase life expectancy while improving the quality of life for individuals of all ages; and
- To eliminate health disparities experienced by individuals because of race, ethnicity, gender, education, income, disability, locality, and sexual orientation

Even in the face of improvements in the overall health of the nation, Americans from racial and ethnic minority groups are still more likely than whites to have poor health and, as a result, to die prematurely. All indicators make it clear that these groups will make up a larger proportion of the U.S. population. As a result, the number of people affected by disparities in healthcare will only increase, so the primary objective of REACH 2010 was to help communities mobilize resources to support programs that addressed these disparities.

The racial and ethnic groups targeted by the REACH 2010 project were African Americans, American Indians, Alaska Natives, Asian Americans, Hispanics, and Pacific Islanders. The REACH 2010 Project had six health priority areas: infant mortality; breast and cervical cancer screening and management; cardiovascular disease; diabetes; child and adult immunization; and HIV/AIDS.

REACH 2010 was initially designed as a two-phased, five-year demonstration project to support community coalitions in the design, implementation, and evaluation of community-based strategies to eliminate health disparities. Phase I was a twelve-month planning period that involved a competitive application process that awarded grants to thirty-two community coalitions to develop a community action plan. Phase II provided twenty-four of the initial community grantees with implementation grants.

In 1998, before the launch of the REACH 2010 initiative, CHC, Inc. brought together key stakeholders in South Los Angeles and established the African Americans Building a Legacy of Health Collaborative (AABLH) in an effort to raise the community's awareness of and role in addressing the growing disparity in health within the African American community. The effort resulted in a truly unique gathering of strength within the African American community in Los Angeles to address the crisis. For the first time, organizations such as the American Diabetes Association, the American Heart Association, the Los Angeles County Department of Health Services, Long Beach Department of Health And Human Services, public health and urban planning researchers from the University of Southern California and UCLA, church-based networks, the State Department of Health Services nutrition and chronic disease divisions, as well as a broad range of African American community-based health and community development organizations came together to create a unified voice and force in the community.

In 1999, with a one-year planning grant from the CDC, the AABLH Collaborative went to work on developing a community action plan for specific communities in Los Angeles County. The following parameters were agreed and with the REACH 2010 implementation grant, acted upon:

- Cardiovascular disease and diabetes within the African American community, targeting neighborhoods within the cities of Inglewood, Compton, South Los Angeles, and Long Beach with the highest concentration of African Americans and offering a broad economic profile of the African American community in Los Angeles County.
- Physical activity and nutrition as significant risk factors for CVD and diabetes. Fundamental to the plan was the linking of the underlying issues of racism, economics, and culture, with behavioral and physiological risk factors attributed to cardiovascular disease and diabetes. Three strategic directions provide the framework of the action plan, each designed to support the other.
- Recreating Community Norms through Education and Prevention: activities designed to increase the social and organizational support system within the African American community for creating a healthier lifestyle.
- Economic Parity Through Community Development: activities designed to increase access to those resources that improve the health status of the community.
- Policy and Institutional Change Through Community Empowerment: activities designed to increase the community's authority and role in addressing the issue of racism and those policies that regulate behavior or delivery of services in order to achieve improved health outcomes.
- In an effort to address the root cause of disease in the African American community, the community action plan was developed to go beyond conventional intervention practices and create a system of

support for at-risk individuals and accountability for the health, nutrition, and environmental resources in the community.

A. Implementation Approach

We utilized community-based participatory research because of its focus on social, structural, and physical environmental inequities through active involvement on community members, organizational representatives, and researchers in all aspects of the research process (Israel et al. 1998). The underlying goal of the project was to reduce CVD and diabetes through creating an environment for healthier living for the underserved African American communities (target areas) in Los Angeles County. The model consisted of:

- Creating assessment instruments and inventories, evaluating the resource environments of the target areas, and conducting additional assessments in more affluent communities in West Los Angeles (comparison area) to show the health disparities between the communities
- Developing community/organizational wellness programs to encourage healthy eating and structured physical activity, and assessing the organizational and individual changes through the programs
- Conducting general and targeted education programs to inform residents and healthcare providers of the target areas about the targeted condition
- Piloting support groups to aid people diagnosed with the targeted condition.

B. Key REACH 2010 Findings and Lessons Learned

1. CHC/AABLH Collaborative Effective in Role of Change Agent

Individuals from public, private, and non-profit sector organizations were asked to engage in one or more activities to make it easier for individuals in the target communities to make healthier choices. The majority of the participants supported the direction of the CHC/AABLH project and believed that the project had a positive impact on CVD and diabetes through developing (and enhancing) nutrition and physical activity resources in the targeted communities.

2. CHC/AABLH Collaborative Instrumental in Increasing Awareness of and Accessing Community Resources for Healthy Living

The CHC/AABLH project has been able to get a diverse group of individuals and organizations engaged in efforts to increase the quality and accessibility of nutrition and physical activity resources in the targeted communities. Various means—MOUS, mini-grants to support projects by a variety of community and faith-based organizations, advisory committees—allowed stakeholders to increase their awareness of existing resources, and engage in processes that led to increases in resources available in the community.

3. CHC/AABLH Collaborative Community Resources for Healthy Living Differ from Other Communities

The target areas were significantly less likely to have important food items and physical activity facilities or programs for living a healthier life than the comparison area. The variety and quality of healthy food in markets, the quality and preparation of healthy food in restaurants, and the quantity and quality of physical activity facilities and programs were significantly lower in the target areas.

4. CHC/AABLH Collaborative Shows the Benefit of Bringing Resources for Healthy Living to the Community

The physical activity mini-grant program was very successful in getting diverse people (men, seniors, women), diverse places (churches, clinics, public housing facilities), and diverse programs (basketball, dance, swimming) engaged in physical activity.

   In addition, individuals that participated in organizational wellness programs showed significant changes in eating behaviors and mental and physical health conditions among the long-term (twelve-week) participants compared to the short-term (six-week) participants. In addition, participants in general and targeted education sessions, and in project support groups, indicated that they learned a lot about diabetes, cardiovascular disease, and other medical conditions through the programs.

V. The REACH US Project 2007–2012

In 2007 the CDC initiated its REACH US program. With these funds, they established eighteen Centers of Excellence in the Elimination of Disparities, and twenty-two Action Communities. CHC was the recipient of an Action Community Grant, and continued its work in South Los Angeles. The intended beneficiaries of the CHC/AABLH REACH US

Project efforts were the residents, public, private, and non-profit organizations, elected officials, and other policy makers in South Los Angeles. The intent was to engage each of these South Los Angeles stakeholders in efforts to improve or develop nutrition and physical activity resources in the community.

The overarching goal of the CHC/AABLH REACH US Health Project was to improve access to quality nutritious food and physical activity opportunities through institutional practices, public policy, and local reinvestment. The achievement of this goal was broken down into the following two goals:

- Goal 1: Improve access to quality, nutritious food opportunities in South LA through policies that change institutional practices, improve existing resources, and promote local reinvestment
- Goal 2: Improve access to physical activity opportunities in South LA through policies that change institutional practices, improve existing resources, and promote local reinvestment

We utilized community-based participatory research because of its focus on social, structural, and physical environmental inequities through active involvement of community members, organizational representatives, and researchers in all aspects of the research process (Israel et al. 1999). The project consisted of:

1 Using assessment instruments and inventories to evaluate the resource environments of South Los Angeles County, and conducting additional assessments in more affluent communities in West Los Angeles (comparison area) to show the health disparities between the communities
2 Using the assessments to generate a dialogue between the relevant stakeholders that ultimately leads to the joint development of community priorities and policies
3 Documenting the process of community activation and the development of policies and practices that improve the resource environments in South Los Angeles, recognizing this as a necessary condition for the improvement of health outcomes in South Los Angeles

The majority of the program interventions and materials were initially developed with REACH 2010 funds. In relation to interventions, they flowed from elements of the initial funding that were the most successful and also most highly valued by project participants. In relation to materials, this included strategies for community outreach and education, assessment instruments for markets, restaurants, and physical activity sites, and tools for documenting partner participation. Each of these interventions and materials were revised during the REACH US project, including additional nutritional and physical activity resources seen as more relevant by community partners. Such additions include the focus on expired food, additional elements of the physical environment, and also a concern for social capital issues.

The three overarching evaluation questions surrounding nutrition and physical activity resources in South Los Angeles were:

1   Did we improve opportunities for nutrition and physical activity in the South Los Angeles focus areas?
2   Did we establish new or expand existing associations in the South Los Angeles focus areas?
3   Did we work together to take action?

It should be noted at the outset that the answer to each of these questions is yes—nutritional and physical activity resources have improved in South Los Angeles, and this is in part the result of a concerted effort by the CHC/AABLH projects to develop a dynamic network of diverse stakeholders who were willing to invest personal and/or professional resources in either protecting and/or improving existing resources or incentivizing new resources coming into South Los Angeles.

A. Key REACH US Findings and Results

1. Nutrition Interventions

AABLH was successful in achieving its overall five-year goal of nutritious food access improvement as part of comprehensive strategies to reduce CVD, and diabetes disparities with the following policy, environmental, and systems changes.

Policy: Interim Control Ordinance two-year moratorium on new fast food restaurant development; amendment to the LA General Plan instituting an administrative footnote permanently regulating the density of new free-standing fast food restaurant development in South LA.

New Community Plan draft released in fall of 2012 for Baldwin Hills/Adams/Leimert Park contains language that restricts fast food restaurant development near schools, as well as language that extends restaurant density requirements to include transit-oriented districts. For the first time in LA history, the implementation plan for the new Community Plan document includes provisions for CHC's proposed Healthy Restaurant Incentive Program and zoning incentives for grocery store development in the designated region.

Environmental: As result of the increased discourse on fresh food access spurred by the AABLH consortium, during this grant period from 2007 to 2012 there have been seven new grocery stores established in the profiled region, three area neighborhood markets are undergoing healthy food transformations, and funding for two additional South LA neighborhood market conversions has been secured through the FreshWorks Fund. CHC also co-chairs a subsidiary group of the LA Food Policy Council that is working to develop an incentive-based policy that supports Neighborhood Market Conversions throughout the City. Furthermore, three local farmers' markets were established, new community gardens in the profiled area were created, and a food cooperative is in development.

Systems: Creation of California FreshWorks Food Financing Fund to encourage new food retail establishment in communities with inadequate nutrition resources. The program not only provides financing for the development of new grocery stores in underserved communities but also incorporates and promotes the adoption of standards for fresh produce.

Changes in Built Environment Trends in 2007–2012: Only one new stand-alone fast food restaurant was developed in a restricted area. Seven new grocery stores opened since 2007, and between 2010 and 2012 there was more than a 50 percent reduction in the South LA portion of the County's fast food restaurant permits. There were three neighborhood store conversions, three newly established farmers' markets in the area, and one food cooperative developed during this period.

2. Physical Activity Interventions

AABLH made significant progress towards its overall five-year goal of physical activity opportunity access improvement as part of comprehensive strategies to reduce CVD and diabetes disparities with the following policy, environmental, and systems changes.

Policy: adoption of Community Standards District (CSD) overlay zone for unprecedented regulation of oil drilling operations in a recreational area in an otherwise park-poor and densely populated region, to improve the safety of adjacent parkland and facilitate park expansion.

Environmental: as a result of the increased discourse spawned by AABLH's Coalition for an Active South Los Angeles and its Re-imagining Empty Space Tour and Summit, the foundation has been laid for policy on re-purposing unused publicly owned spaces.

Systems: establishment of a citizen advisory panel to oversee the oil drilling operator's compliance with provisions of the CSD; the creation of a regulatory agency panel to oversee the oil drilling operator's compliance with provisions of the CSD. Before the adoption of the CSD there were no annual limits on the number of new or redrilled wells. Since adoption and following protections granted in the 2011 Settlement Agreement, the oil operator is limited to thirty-five new or re-drilled wells annually. Furthermore, the oil field operator is no longer able to operate an unlimited number of drill rigs at any one time; the limit has been reduced to two drill rigs.

Before the CSD, the county had no obligations to facilitate well closures or manage well abandonment. Since the CSD and Settlement Agreement, incentives have been granted to close wells near the perimeter of the oil fields near homes, significantly reducing resident exposure to field operations and potential impacts. The CSD and Settlement Agreement mandated for the first time that the County must perform Community Health Assessments with environmental justice components every five years throughout the life of the CSD.

B. Media Coverage

Using media coverage as an estimate of the potential reach of the CHC/AABLH project, the project has reached at least sixty million people. This estimate is based on April 2012 coverage by New America Media, on work that CHC and its partners is doing around 'fracking' by PXP in the Baldwin Hills area. New America Media states that it reaches over sixty million ethnic minorities through its TV, radio, online, print, and mobile partners.

Additional, more conservative estimates of the potential reach of the CHC/AABLH project would have to examine coverage on multiple international, national, state, and local media sites. For example, in 2008 MacLeans Canada, with its 2.4 million subscribers, did an article on the early work around the South Los Angeles Food Moratorium, calling it a "provocative social experiment ... the first to ban fast food for public health reasons". Kington and Köhler state: "And this 83-sq.-km district that's home to 720,000, mostly black and Hispanic, 28 per cent of whom live below the poverty line, would appear to present the *perfect test case:* nowhere is the twinning of super-sized meals and super-sized people more overt" (italics added). Other online sources include the Jubilee Consortium, Reporting on Health (10,280 followers) and South LA Connected, both efforts of the Annenberg School of Communication, and SoCal Connected, a KCET product.

Stories on the CHC/AABLH work on the food and physical activity environments in South Los Angeles have been covered by local TV stations KCBS/KCAL (2011–2012 Nielsen average 11.75 million viewers), KNBC (7.41 million viewers), Univision (3.63 million viewers), and KTLA (1.72 million viewers). Radio coverage has included KPCC, Swedish Public Radio, and Annenberg Radio. Multiple newspapers, ranging in weekly readerships of 34,000 for the *Merced Sun Star* to over 4.3 million for the *LA Times*, further extends the potential reach of the CHC/AABLH project. From 2007–2012 at least one story a year was read, viewed, heard, or downloaded on the CHC/AABLH project.

VI. Conclusions on the CHC Model for Change

No matter the cause of the inequity, action is required to address the problems that continue to lead to disability and premature death, and CHC answered that call to action. Using a bottom-up approach, CHC and its partners used community-based assessments of health supportive resources as a primary vehicle for building community awareness, community capacity, and ultimately policy advocacy. Community residents and community-based organizations were invited to do the various assessments, trained in how to do the assessments, and then asked to present the results of the assessments (along with sharing their collective experiences as they surveyed the resources) (Sloane et al., 2006).

As community residents shared the results, the differences between resources in South Los Angeles and West Los Angeles were magnified (Lewis et al., 2005). Differences that were 'common knowledge' in the community were given the additional credibility gained from the research process and the subsequent publication of the results in top-tier research journals. As the audience for the results expanded, CHC and its partners were in a position to lead discussions on possible solutions and implement those solutions.

The evaluation findings overwhelmingly support the notion that the CHC Model for Change is an effective strategy for engaging a diverse group of stakeholders, over an extended period of time, in solving nutrition and physical activity issues at the local level. By having community-based (or linked) stakeholders engaged in all stages of the process, opportunities for a strong community voice and community-directed action were sustained throughout the extended project period of 1999–2012. Assessments, focus groups, interviews, and coalition activities have led to new and improved nutrition resources being added to South Los Angeles, and the ground work has been laid for comparable resource improvement regarding physical activity.

Several conclusions and lessons learned can be drawn from the CHC/ AABLH project activities that are noteworthy for others interested in community-led change efforts. First, community-led change must involve 'structured flexibility'. In particular, it was clear that the CHC/AABLH project had a path it wanted the community to follow related to nutrition and physical activity. However, the project also maintained enough flexibility to respond to windows of opportunity—unanticipated chances for a stronger community voice in evolving local nutrition and physical activity related issues.

Second, finding partners in community-based change means focusing on common areas of interest and what such partners can do, not the wholesale adoption of everything that partners might want to do in the community, or making demands of organizations outside of the scope of what they can legitimately do. More directly, the success in the CHC/

AABLH project can be linked to the time it took to engage stakeholders in ongoing discussions and targeted actions around what would be a 'win' for each of them and the constituencies that they represented.

Finally, it is critical to note the importance of the ongoing dialogue for all the stakeholders in the community change process. Relationship building requires trust and communication. While not perfect, the CHC/ AABLH project made significant progress in being seen as an entity that delivers on its promises and keeps relevant stakeholders informed. Table 10.2 provides a summary of the major project milestones through 2012.

Table 10.2 CHC Model for Change—AABLH Project Milestones (1999–2012)

Model Phase
Catalyst
Health Disparities in South Los Angeles
Inequities in Resource Environments as Contributing Factor
Coalition Building
AABLH Coalition Established
AABLH Coalition Recruitment
AABLH Coalition Meetings
Issues and Values Identification
AABLH Community Action Plan Development
Strategic Directions Established
AABLH Coalition Expansion
AABLH Coalition Meetings
Community Based Assessment
Development of Mini-Grant Award Process
Review and Awarding of Mini-Grants
Survey Training for Community Groups Awarded Mini-Grants
Data Collection: Markets, Restaurants, Physical Activity Sites
Neighborhood Food Watch
Data Presentations by Community Groups
AABLH Coalition Meetings
Policy and Program Development
Community Forums—Data Release
Production of Policy Briefs
Journal Publications
Media Coverage
Meetings with Elected Officials—City, County, State, and Federal Levels
Meetings with Public Agencies—Health, Planning, Development, Parks and Recreation, Transportation

Model Phase
Meetings with Grocers
Meetings with Oil Company
AABLH Coalition Meetings
Market Opportunities—Incentives for Food Retailers Enacted
Fast Food Interim Control Ordinance (ICO) Enacted
Food Desert Symposium
Re-Imagining Space Symposium
Community Standards District Enacted (Oilfields)
Policy and Program Implementation
Market Opportunities—Incentives for Food Retailers Adoption and Impact
Fast Food Interim Control Ordinance (ICO) Adoption and Impact
Community Standards District Adoption and Impact
South Los Angeles General Plan Amendment/Footnote Adopted
Proposed Revisions to South Los Angeles General Plans

References

Berkowitz, B., and T. Wolff. 2000. *The Spirit of the Coalition*. Washington, DC: American Public Health Association.

Centers for Disease Control and Prevention. The social-ecological model: a framework for prevention. http://www.cdc.gov/ViolencePrevention/overview/social-ecologicalmodel.html (update March 2015; last accessed April 2, 2016).

Israel, B. A., A. J. Schultz, and A. B. Becker. 1998. Review of community based research: Accessing partnership approaches to improve public health. *Annual Review of Public Health* 19: 173–202.

Kawachi, I., S.V. Subramanian, and N. Almeida-Filho. 2002. A glossary for health inequalities. *Journal of Epidemiol Community Health*. 56: 647–652.

Kingdon, J.W. *Agendas, Alternatives, and Public Policies*. 2nd ed. 1995. New York, NY: Longman.

Lewis L.B., L. Galloway-Gilliam, G. Flynn et al. 2011. Transforming the urban food desert from the grassroots up: A model for community change. *Family and Community Health*. 34 Suppl. 1: S92-S101.

Lewis, L. B., D. C. Sloane, L. M. Nascimento et al. 2005. African Americans' access to healthy food options in south Los Angeles restaurants. *American Journal of Public Health* 95: 668–202.

McLeroy K.R., D. Bibeau, A. Steckler, and K. Glanz. 1988. An ecological perspective on health promotion programs. *Health Education Quarterly* 15(4):351–377.

National Center for Injury Prevention and Control, Division of Violence Prevention. http://www.cdc.gov/ViolencePrevention/overview/social-ecologicalmodel.html. Updated March 25, 2015. Accessed April 2, 2016.

Sloane D., L. Nascimento, G. Flynn, et al. 2006. Assessing resource environments to target prevention interventions in community chronic disease control. *Journal of Health Care Poor Underserved* 17(2 Suppl): 146–158.

Sloane D., A.L. Diamant, L.B. Lewis et al. 2003. Improving the nutritional resource environment for healthy living through community-based participatory research. *Journal of General Internal Medicine* 8(7): 568–575.

Part IV

Leadership Practices to Address Social Determinants and Population Health

11 Chapter Themes for Leadership Best Practices

Richard F. Callahan, DPA

I. Introduction

A set of leadership themes emerges consistently across each of the preceding chapters. These themes suggest a set of effective leadership practices for addressing the social determinants of health and for advancing population health. These leadership practices developed from the cases and examples in each chapter are specifically targeted to supporting the reader in getting traction on change—now or in the future—in your location, in your department or organization, in your neighborhood or community, in the public policies that impact the health of those you serve now or will serve. As noted in the case of the Institute for Population Health Improvement, there is "purposeful" action to effect change. The cases provide examples of what "purposeful" looks like in practice, and how you operationalize intent.

These leadership lessons can be seen as how to move off of the path dependencies that are both societal and intensely local as noted by Nobel Laureate Douglass North (1990) in economics and Putnam (1993) in sociology in contemporary society in institutions and organizations. More recently, Gladwell (2015) reviews a range of sociological research that looks at the impact of the Hurricane Katrina diaspora, finding that individual outcomes—particularly for lower economic earners—are profoundly shaped by the paths set through living in their neighborhood. The complexities of changing path dependencies defy easy solutions and cross the research boundaries of any one academic discipline. Recognizing the need for multi-disciplinary approaches has been at the core of this book.

Drawing on multiple sources of actionable research, this chapter unfolds by listing six sets of leadership practices, with each set drawing on specific references from one or more of the chapters, as well connecting the reader to research findings on leadership from outside the chapters. The leadership themes specific to these cases also share effective practice with research findings from outside the social determinants of health and population health.

II. Professional Career Experience Matters

The first leadership lesson that emerges is that professional experience matters. Powerful new ideas and better practices emerge from a lifetime of engagement, with a deep understanding of the complexities of the challenges in addressing the social determinants of health and improving population health.

The individual journeys of each of the authors facilitated the development of a range of skills and the passion or core values driving their refusal to accept the world as they found it. There is no sense of stumbling into a way forward. The career trajectories of the authors of each chapter prepared them for the significant challenges of addressing the social determinants of health, and for developing opportunities in a turbulent health landscape. For several of the authors, such as Kizer, Iton, Ross, and Chet Hewitt, their current leadership practices emerged from experiences in both the public and nonprofit sectors, as well as at different levels of government. This experience in both the nonprofit and public sectors provided insight into the strengths and limitations of each sector, as well as an understanding of where there could be intersections for working together on new approaches, new programs.

The complexities encountered to move away from path dependencies call for a deep understanding of the range of moving parts. In drawing on their more than twenty years of experience, each of the authors is better able to account for the wide range of moving parts and people involved in the change processes. Similarly, for the researchers, Lavonna Blair Lewis and Dru Bhattacharya draw on more than twenty years of professional experience in researching and writing about approaches for innovation.

However, this does not mean that early career professionals cannot begin a journey with great impact. In a familiar example, while attending Harvard Medical School Dr. Paul Farmer shows an inspiring case of early career impact in the central highlands of Haiti (Kidder, 2003). Similarly, Michael Marmot (2015) describes asking questions early in his career, which led to his journey to focus on the study of and a career in addressing the social determinants of health. Rather, the leadership lessons suggest a premium on a career trajectory that addresses the most challenging of issues.

III. Focus on Impact: Embrace Accountability

In each chapter, the leaders embrace accountability in the community for the impact of new initiatives. In leadership practice, Bob Biller, former Vice Provost and Dean at the University of Southern California, spoke of leaders as having an impact on two factors: space and time. In each of these chapters the accountability addresses these two features. The first area of space for impact jumps out from these cases, with each chapter focused on place-based health improvements. For the California Endowment in Boyle Heights, for MLP in Chicago, healthy nutrition for South Central Los Angeles, and other cases, the leaders choose the space to have impact–not in an amorphous or generalized sense but in a clearly defined location, with specified expected impacts.

The second leadership influence is on time. In each of these cases, the leader's commitment to accountability is across three dimensions: at the front end of the process, during the programs, and at the back end. Initially each program develops a deep understanding of the community needs. As discussed in the next practice, this assessment relies on quantitative assessments of health needs. This assessment translated into targeted programs. Each of the leaders embraced accountability in a formalized assessment, through formal program evaluation.

IV. Dive Deep Into the Data

At the start of each leadership journey into addressing an aspect of the social determinants of health you find a deep dive into the data. In advancing population health, IPHI develops data on cancer mortality and across a range of engagements throughout the state of California; in Building Healthy Communities the chapter focuses on the data for health disparities in Boyle Heights for East Los Angeles; for the community health needs assessment in Chicago the numbers start with asthma; in Sacramento the data is infant mortality for African American children; and in South Central Los Angeles the numbers are on nutrition and activity. Each chapter builds a case for change through quantitative analysis. The leaders in each chapter find the numbers that matter and then begin the search for leverage points to change the negative indicators.

The research in each of the chapters avoids what Lavonna Blair Lewis has described as "drive-by research". Rather than dropping in on a community to study patterns, the researchers, in the case of Lavonna Blair Lewis with the Community Health Councils and Dru Bhattacharya as advisor and researcher for the Health Justice Project, have a longstanding commitment to the community being researched. Similarly, with the Sierra Health Foundation, the California Endowment, and the Los Angeles County Department of Public Health, their analytics are precursors to action with the community.

However, the leadership lesson does not end with finding the initial data. Rather, consistently in each of the chapters, the initial analytics are not only a precursor to action but begin a process of measurement, with more data, and quantitative as well as qualitative assessment designed into the process. In this way, data not only drives the initial efforts but informs adjustments along the journey, as well as driving future change.

| New Sources | → | Endowed Sources | → | Public Sources |
| Social Impact Bonds | | Foundations | | Public Agencies |

Figure 11.1 Funding Continuum

V. Financing Takes Different Forms

The leadership practices in the chapters suggest that financing takes different forms, not limited to traditional public sector funding or intergovernmental funding. There is a range of funding sources described, from the most speculative, in the form of social impact bounds described in Chapter 5, to the most predictable, found in Chapter 2 for funding public agencies. This range suggests visualizing a continuum, as in Figure 11.1.

A second theme is the role of the philanthropic sector beyond acting as the funder of nonprofits. What emerges in several of the cases is philanthropy as a fourth sector, in addition to the public, nonprofit, and for profit sectors. In this way the philanthropic sector leaders can be seen as funding that serves as a catalyst for change.

VI. Partnerships for Traction

A consistent leadership practice through each of the chapters is the development of partnerships. Problem solving through collaboration is a recognized development in the social sector, starting with Provan and Milward's (1995) groundbreaking research on networks in mental health to contemporary and long-standing research noting the expansive role of networks to the extent that to manage in the public sector is to collaborate through networks (Agranoff, 2012). The contribution in each chapter is twofold: first, a set of practices that helps identify community needs through networks; and second, the leadership practices in finance and strategy that develops new networks, and connects with—but does not displace—existing networks.

In each chapter, an operating premise can be seen in that addressing the social determinants of health and population health needs cannot be done alone, whether via a public organization, nonprofit, or philanthropy. Partnerships are recognized throughout the book as significant ways to connect with the community, as well as mechanisms for getting traction on change. More specifically, the leaders operationalized collaboration through three types of approaches:

1   Innovating new approaches
2   Leveraging the intergovernmental system
3   Developing cross-sectoral partnership

Again, as with financing, there is no one way to proceed; rather, different approaches are adapted to the specifics of community needs. As previewed in the introduction to this book, there is not an orthodoxy presented. Instead, aligned with Elinor Ostrom's (2010) research on the emergence of voluntary cooperation, the guiding practice for successful outcomes is local adaptation. In this way, partnerships are very much nested in other leadership practices, including a career trajectory that builds understanding and credibility, approaches driven by a deep dive into the data, incorporating measures for accountability, varied funding mechanisms, and purposefulness through strategy development.

VII. Strategy Designs Success

Each of the preceding five lessons then informed the development of strategy. Success is by design, not by accident. The steps taken are not random, hoping for a positive outcome, nor relying on luck or a cascading effect to bring attention to the problem. As described by Jim Collins (2011) in his research on private sector companies' responses to the Great Recession of 2008, leadership choices make the difference, not the environment. Strategy in each of these chapters most basically connects the organization to the environment in which it operates, designating or obtaining assets, and then assigning steps to achieve agreed-upon outcomes. The leaders in each chapter advance individual and population health through the data, financing, partnerships, and formal evaluation, informing strategy development that creates accountability for positive change.

Across each of the chapters the successes occur by design, not by accident. As noted by Chet Hewitt in his efforts to reduce African American child mortality, there is an intentionality in the approach—or as expressed by the Institute for Population Health Improvement, there is a "purposefulness". A strategy deeply informed by professional experience underpinned the range of initiatives recounted in the varied chapters, whether in developing new organizations (Dr. Ken Kizer at the Institute for Population Health Improvement), sharing with other authors who were redirecting existing organizations (Dr. Iton and Dr. Ross at the California Endowment, and Jon Freedman at LA County Department of Public Health), or developing new partnerships (Chet Hewitt at Sierra Health Foundation and Lavonna Blair Lewis). As noted by Dr. Kizer at IHPI, population health management is defined as "taking purposeful actions" (IHPI, 2016), so that purposeful and intentional strategy development is inherent in addressing population health needs. Consistent with findings in the private sector during the 2008 economic downturn (Collins, 2011), success is not a function of luck or a favorable environment; rather, success is a function of disciplined decision-making, aligned with a well-developed but adaptive strategy, resulting in measurable outcomes.

162 *Richard F. Callahan*

The leadership choices, decision-making, and strategy account for positive outcomes, as opposed to the environment or lucky choices. An important part of this strategy is long-term commitments. For example, the California Endowment *Building Health Communities* is a ten-year effort. The other partnerships are built on long-standing relationships and reputations. Each of the initiatives recounted in the chapters exhibit what Nobel Prize-winning political scientist Elinor Ostrom (1990) termed "credible commitment". The partners with each of the authors could look at a set of long-standing and demonstrated commitments to addressing significant aspects related to the social determinants of health, public health, quality healthcare, health access, and innovation.

VIII. Conclusion

Though listed as six sets of practices in a sequence, this does not imply that each practice stands alone. Rather, similar to Ostrom (1990) describing her research findings, these practices are nested within each other. For example, strategy development draws on career experiences and partnership development as leadership practice includes embracing accountability. The nested quality of these practices again reflects the complexity of addressing the range of moving parts and people involved in the social determinants of health and population health improvements.

The chapters describe, in many cases from the inside out, how leaders actually address complex social challenges. These are not speculative or aspirational leadership practices. Many of the chapters describe how these leaders see the world in their own words. Furthermore, these leadership chapters include what the leaders themselves see as the important steps from the inside, from their positions of leadership. The chapters include the world views that shape their practices and how they operationalize change.

The challenges addressed in this book are not going away. Moreover, even when healthcare practices that emphasize quality care are in place, the unfortunate example of the Veterans Health Administration in 2012 provides a cautionary tale of how a system can unravel with tragic consequences (Kizer and Jha, 2014). Rather, the work to address the social determinants of health has in many ways begun over past decades, not only in the regions described in this book but also across the world (Kidder, 2003; Marmot, 2015). The leadership practices identified in this book are intended to support communities and public health leaders in continuing to get traction on the many moving parts, to address social inequities and the current path dependencies that devastate community and individual health. Moreover, this book intends to model the practice of finding what works in one community and sharing that with a wider range of practitioners, researchers, and teachers, working to address the social determinants of health and advance population health.

Each of these chapters captures what Chet Hewitt as President of Sierra Health Foundation has found throughout his career in the public and philanthropic sectors: "...that there is nothing as powerful as a good idea" (Callahan, 2015). Each of the chapters presents good ideas coupled with the leadership practices that facilitate getting traction on those good ideas. These leadership practices are in great demand. After four decades of research on leadership and advising world leaders, Warren Bennis noted the urgent need for leadership to anticipate "... the four most important threats facing the world today: (a) a nuclear or biological catastrophe, whether deliberate or accidental; (b) a world-wide epidemic; (c) tribalism and its cruel offspring, assimilation (all three of these are more likely than they were a decade ago); and finally, (d) the leadership of our human institutions" (2007: 4). These threats continue to challenge leaders in public health. The chapters offer the good ideas and leadership practices needed to lead human institutions and address each of the challenges highlighted by Warren Bennis. The next step is for you as the reader to adapt these lessons, use them as catalysts for new good ideas, and address the social determinants of health and population health needs in your community.

References

Agranoff, R. 2012. *Collaborating to Manage: A Primer for the Public Sector.* Washington, DC: Georgetown University Press.

Bennis, W. 2007. The challenges of leadership in the modern world. *American Psychologist.* 62(1): 1–4.

Callahan, R. 2015. Innovations at Sierra Health Foundation: Leadership and partnerships to address the social determinants of health. In E. Gibson and P. Julnes (Eds.), *Innovation in the Public and Nonprofit Sectors: A Public Solutions Handbook.* New York: Routledge, pp. 187–204.

Collins, J. 2011. *Great by Choice: Uncertainty, Chaos, and Luck—Why Some Thrive Despite Them All.* New York: HarperCollins.

Gladwell, M. 2015. Starting over: Many Katrina victims left New Orleans for good. What can we learn from them? *The New Yorker.* August 24.

Institute for Population Health Improvement. http://www.ucdmc.ucdavis.edu/iphi/abouttemp.html (accessed 15 August 2016).

Kidder, T. 2003. *Mountains Beyond Mountains: Healing the World: The Quest of Dr. Paul Farmer.* New York: Random House.

Kizer, K. W. and A. K. Jha. 2014. Restoring trust in VA health care. *New England Journal of Medicine* 371(4): 295–297.

Marmot, M. 2015. *The Health Gap: The Challenge of an Unequal World.* London: Bloomsbury.

North, D. 1990. *Institutions, Institutional Change, and Economic Performance.* New York: Cambridge University Press.

Ostrom, E. 1990. *Governing the Commons: The Evolution for Collective Action.* Cambridge: Cambridge University Press.

Ostrom, E. 2010. Beyond markets and states: polycentric governance of complex economic systems. *American Economic Review* 100(3): 641–72.

Provan, K. G. and H. B. Milward. 1995. A preliminary theory of network effectiveness: A comparative study of four community health systems. *Administrative Science Quarterly* 40(1): 1–33.

Putnam, R. 1993. *Making Democracy Work: Civic Traditions in Italy*. Princeton, NJ: Princeton University Press.

Index

Printed in the United States
by Baker & Taylor Publisher Services